C000224727

BET YOU DIDN'T KNOW THIS ABOUT BEIRUT!

Text: Warren Singh-Bartlett
Illustration & Design: Sinan Hallak

turningpoint
BOOKS

Published by:

Turning Point Books

15th Floor, Concorde Building, Dunan Street,
Verdun, Beirut, Lebanon
P.O. Box: 14-6613   Tel: 00961 1 752 100

www.tpbooksonline.com

First edition: December 2010

Text: Warren Singh-Bartlett
Illustration: Sinan Hallak
Layout and graphic design: Sinan Hallak
Editing: Dina Dabbous

ISBN: 978-9953-0-1926-0

Printing:
⊜dots

WE ARE...

THE AUTHOR

Warren Singh-Bartlett first came to Lebanon in 1998 for just three days to see the Three B's: Beirut, Byblos, and Baalbak. Falling in love with the land, he ended up staying somewhat longer than originally planned. Thirteen years, to be precise. He lives in an orange and blue rooftop apartment in a crowded part of Beirut from which he enjoys expansive views into his neighbours living, dining and bathrooms. Luckily, his terrace is heavily vegetated.

Singh-Bartlett is the Middle East correspondent for *Wallpaper* magazine and a contributor to many other publications including *Tank*, London's *Financial Times*, the *New York Times, American Express Departures* magazine, Germany's *Handelsblatt*, and the *DestinAsian* travel magazine. He is currently working on three other book projects because he is easily distracted and has never been much good at finishing things.

THE ILLUSTRATOR / DESIGNER

Lebanese illustrator, Sinan Hallak was born in 1980 in Beirut – the city he always comes home to after his sporadic adventures abroad. He is a graduate of the Lebanese Academy of Fine Arts, ALBA, and between his travels and book projects, Hallak inspires budding young artists in Beirut as a part-time university lecturer.

Hallak is a perceptive illustrator who was particularly drawn to *Bet You Didn't Know This About Beirut;* which he compares to "a good Tabbouleh, intended to be enjoyed by locals and foreigners alike."

INSIDE:

1 OUR ENVIRONMENT

From the exact size of the country and the rarest of Lebanese houseplants to the mysterious creature that terrorised Beirut's answer to Beverley Hills, Our Environment is all about the natural wealth – animal, vegetable and mineral – that surrounds us.

IS Lebanon an Arab country or a country with an Arab face? It sounds like hair-splitting but the Lebanese have disagreed about this definition for decades. Whether it's for reasons of culture, history, tradition or sheer snobbery, there are some Lebanese who like to think of themselves, much like the old Alexandrians, as being in but not of the Middle East.

Before you dismiss this as nonsense, the conceit has scientific support. As the northernmost extension of the Great Rift Valley, the Bekaa Valley doesn't only divide Lebanon from Syria, it also marks the boundary between two of the Earth's tectonic plates. Lebanonists, take heart, as you suspected all along, your country isn't part of Arabia at all. You're part of Africa instead.

N ext time you swing by the garden centre looking for some rare and exotic houseplant, why not try asking for a Lebanese orchid? Yes, you read right, Lebanon has orchids and they're not from some houseplant left to run wild, either. Lebanon is home to 14 indigenous species of orchid including two varieties, the *Orchis Morio-Libani* and the *Orchis Romana-Libanotica,* that are specific to Mount Lebanon. Much smaller in size than their Asian counterparts, though just as brightly coloured and every bit as sensitive to mistreatment, Lebanon's orchids are currently in danger of dying out completely, as a result of construction in the mountains and public indifference towards the increasing degradation, through pollution, of the wild areas that remain.

One of Lebanon's most cherished myths is that it's possible to ski in the morning and swim in the afternoon. The act itself is physically possible. The slopes at Faraya are only 40 minutes from the coast – 30 if you don't use the brakes – but with the ski-season effectively over by the end of March or the middle of April, bathing in the Mediterranean in early spring, when the water temperature hovers around 17°C and the air temperature is only a few degrees higher, the prospect is something only inebriated college students or those raised north of the Arctic Circle are likely to find appealing.

The classic Lebanese joke that the sea is the only one of the country's neighbours not to have invaded it is not quite correct. Massive tsunamis have swept the Lebanese coast at least four times in the last 8,000 years, thanks to a fault that lies 6 kilometres off the coast. The last time this happened was in 515AD, when the 7.5 Richter earthquake, which claimed up to 250,000 lives on the Eastern Mediterranean, was followed by an equally massive wave that drowned Tripoli and may have doused the fires that broke out in Beirut after the quake but also destroyed what little of the city was still standing. Killer tsunamis have happened on average every 1,500 years, which means we're already overdue. A possible bright side? Every time an event like this has happened, the coast of Lebanon has risen by about a metre.

Ever wondered what was swimming in the sea, say, a hundred million years ago? Haqel is the place to go. In a country otherwise fairly poor when it comes to fossilised remains – apart from the dinosaurs in parliament, anyway – the four fish beds of Haqel are world class and one of the earliest recorded fossil sites, with mentions of fish in the rocks dating back to the 4th Century, when Eusebius, the Bishop of Caesaria, cited them as proof of Noah's flood. As to what you can find apart from fish, Haqel has disgorged Late Cretaceous period worms, squid and prawns as well as the occasional octopus and fragments of plant life.

S ometimes though, it seems *Cedrus Libani* is everywhere. Cigarette packets. Key chains. Bottles of honey. Rolls of hygienic paper. MEA tailfins. T-shirts. Everywhere that is, apart from on Mount Lebanon. True, there is that lovely grove up above Bcharreh, a small forest in Tannourine and a larger one on either side of Barouk, but there are more Lebanese cedars in England, for example, than in Lebanon. Surprised? Don't be. Like the Lebanese themselves, transplanted *Cedrus Libani* thrive in a variety of far-flung places; Canada, New Zealand, California, Australia, even in the foothills of the Himalaya, although there they are outnumbered by the world's only other species of cedar, the *Cedrus Deodara*, like its Levantine cousin, also a sacred tree.

Then there are the Libani subspecies; *Cedrus Libani var. brevifolia* (Cyprus), *Cedrus Libani var. atlantica* (Atlas Mountains) and *Cedrus Libani var. stenocoma* (Turkey). As for Syria, which has quite a few cedars of its own, March 14th partisans will no doubt be relieved to know that the variety that grows there is quite emphatically *Cedrus Libani var. libani*, not *var. syriacus*.

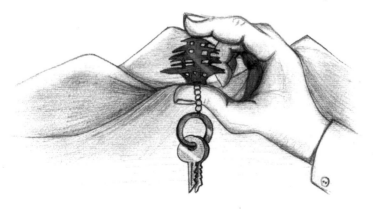

Spend the day in certain parts of town and you're bound to notice a poster somewhere proclaiming that Lebanon's territorial integrity amounts to 10,452 square kilometres. The number, however (in)famous is wrong. Today's Lebanon is larger than that. Thanks to the land reclamations in Dbayeh (1.03 square kilometres) and the new district off the city centre (0.73 square kilometres), that figure should already be revised to 10,453.76. Throw in the dozens of illegal marinas and hotel extensions (at least another square kilometre and a bit between them) and you're probably closer to 10,454.

As for the future, Lebanon can only get bigger. Between the project to extend the Dbayeh landfill all the way down to Beirut port (a further 4 square kilometres) and the more recent but much less palatable plan to reclaim another 3.3 square kilometres from the sea, in the form of a cedar-shaped island off Jiyye, we should eventually reach a figure of 10,461.3. Sound negligible? Perhaps, but in a country so greedily eyed by its neighbours, every square centimetre counts.

Beirut's sole surviving patch of forest, the Horsh Beirut has always existed on the fringes of city life. At first, literally. When it was created by Emir Fakhreddine as a game reserve in the 17th Century, and even when it was enlarged by Ibrahim Pasha in the 19th Century, the Horsh lay kilometres outside the city walls. As it became a pleasure garden in the closing decades of the Ottoman era, the city was drawing closer, but right up to the outbreak of the civil war in 1975, it was so densely forested that for the most part, visitors remained on its edges.

Today, that's all a memory. The trees that weren't cut down for firewood during the war were burned to the ground during an Israeli air raid in 1982, and, while the Horsh was replanted in the early 1990s thanks to French money, it certainly doesn't resemble a forest any more. One thing hasn't changed though. The Horsh is still little-used by Beirutis but these days, that isn't because it's in the middle of nowhere; it's because the city's only green lung is still waiting for its governors to re-open it to the public.

E ver since Phillip Skaff released his eco-tract, *The Republic of Concrete*, it's become fashionable to decry the construction industry's onslaught on Lebanon's mountains. Without wishing to pour oil on Mr. Skaff's troubled waters, or to make light of the country's eco-apocalypse, the complaint isn't original. *The Epic of Gilgamesh*, dated circa 3,000 BC, is the world's earliest known story and part of it details the destruction of the forests of Hermon and Mount Lebanon to build the city of Uruk.

Pretty much all of Lebanon's rulers have taken their axes to its greenery. Even as Isaiah waxed lyrical about the trees of the Lord, the Phoenicians were chopping them down to build their boats. The Egyptians followed suit, making their royal barques, bedsteads, palace furniture and even the odd children's toy out of God's favourite evergreen, and used cedar resin in the embalming process for making mummies. King Ahiram happily sold half of what still grew above Sidon to Solomon, who built his temple in Jerusalem from cedar, and things carried on in this vein until the Romans. Their stripping of the mountains was so thorough and so voracious that it took an Imperial proclamation (Thanks, Hadrian) to stop.

There are crevices high up on the eastern flanks of Mount Lebanon where snow remains throughout the year. Not enough to go skiing, but more than enough for a snow-ball fight in the summer. Lebanon's snow, such an exotic sight in this part of the world, not only gave the country its name, it was also one of its first exports. From ancient times right up until just over a century ago, blocks of ice were carried down the mountain and used to chill the drinks and make the sherbets of pharaohs, princes and sultans from Luxor to Istanbul. That is, until the transatlantic ice trade began in Massachusetts and flooded the world with a cheaper alternative.

Bears. Baboons. Lions. In theory, the trade in wild animals is illegal in Lebanon. In practice, well, let's just say that the right connections or a willingness to pay makes almost anything possible. Take the piranhas that were used as interior décor in a tank in the floor of one former Monot club, for example. The owners clearly didn't figure, or else simply didn't care that, eventually, the starving fish would eat one another. Then there was the case of the lion cub left to starve to death in a cage in Qarantina before it was rescued.

Sometimes though, nature has the last laugh. In 2003, a 2.5 metre long lizard was spotted roaming around the swanky homes of Rabieh. For weeks, it roamed the area, eating pets, digging up dead horses and swimming in neighbourhood pools, including the kiddie pool at the Mtayleb country club. In the end, it turned out the lizard, which some people had thought was a crocodile, was a Komodo Dragon, a rare Indonesian monitor lizard with a taste for goats. It had apparently been abandoned by one of the area's inhabitants and found sustenance snacking on Rabieh's cats and dogs.

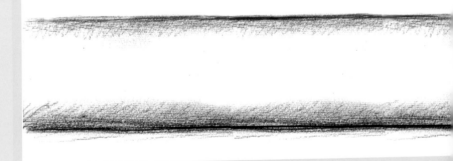

AS crazy as it sounds, two thousand years ago, the inhabitants of Lattakia used to row four kilometres out to sea to collect drinking water. And not from passing ships either, directly from the sea itself. The shore of the Eastern Mediterranean is dotted with freshwater springs that emerge on the seabed. Most release only small amounts of water but some, like the one off Lattakia, are so powerful that the water they release is drinkable. In Lebanon, the best-known sea springs in antiquity were off Batroun and Shekka, but they're still being discovered today, and one found off Tyre in 2009 is powerful enough to be tapped. Over the years, many of Lebanon's sea springs have stopped flowing as their sources have been diverted on land. Others have disappeared under construction. Jal el-Dib once had two sea springs just off the beach, one of which released water that was warm enough to swim in during the winter. Both now bubble somewhere beneath the Beirut-Tripoli highway.

Sometimes beauty is a curse. Just ask Adonis. Having seduced Astarte with his beauty, he was gored to death on a hunting trip in Afqa by a boar sent by the goddess' jealous paramour, Ares. The demigod bled so profusely that he turned the waters of Afqa's river – the Nahr Ibrahim – red, and as he lay dying in his lover's arms, the drops of blood falling from his wound became tiny red blossoms. Those crimson-coloured anemones still carpet Mount Lebanon every spring, and once a year the first snow melt washes ochre-coloured earth into the river, turning it again, a delicate shade of red.

It's no surprise that in a country as inherently contrary as Lebanon, there is a river that seems to defy the laws of Nature herself. Rising in Labweh, about 10 kilometres north-east of the city of Baalbek in the Bekaa Valley, the Orontes River – which is known in Arabic as the Aasi, or rebel river – does not flow directly towards the sea, like almost every other river on the planet. Instead, it heads inland and after meandering casually through northern Syria, it finally meets the sea some 400 kilometres later in southern Turkey.

Given a choice, the Orontes would likely take an easier route but thanks to Lebanon's distinctive geography, it has little choice. The river is cut off from the coast by the eastern flank of Mount Lebanon. Still, as rebels go, the Aasi has been generous. While it isn't very deep or even especially wide, it's been an important source of water for thousands of years and in Roman times, part of its flow was diverted along aqueducts towards the desert kingdom of Palmyra, 150 kilometres to the east.

For all the many metres of snow that blanket the mountains above Beirut each winter, the city rarely sees much snow itself. Sometimes, a combination of hail and sleet are enough to leave a light and fleeting layer of white but the last time Beirut got real snow that lasted more than 5 minutes was in February 1950, when shivering residents woke up to a 6 centimetre blanket that covered the entire eastern Mediterranean from Alexandria to Istanbul. Previous falls had occurred in 1942 and 1920 and apparently happened on average every 20 or 30 years before then. Today, Beirut may simply be too big to allow snow to settle. The heat trap created as the city has become more densely built-up means that it is usually at least 1-3°C warmer than unbuilt stretches of the coastline.

Lebanon has been keeping track of its weather since the middle of the 19th Century, when the Middle East's first observatory – the now-defunct Lee Observatory at the Amercian University of Beirut (AUB) – and a second meteorological station at Universite Saint Joseph (USJ) were established. The country's meteorological department was founded on July 4th 1921, a year after a second observatory had been built by the Jesuits in Ksara. Although record-keeping was patchy and frequently interrupted by Lebanon's political upheavals, by the outbreak of war in 1975, there were 187 information-gathering stations around the country, most of which were destroyed by fighting. To date, the lowest temperature recorded in Lebanon is -22.7°C on January 20th, 1964 in Yammouneh, and the highest, 44.8°C, was recorded in Beirut at the Nazareth School on May 10th, 1941.

G littering crystals. World War II ammunition. Crusader mummies and prehistoric remains, Lebanon's caves are underground treasure troves but the most interesting thing about them may be the extent of their existence. Lebanon is mostly limestone, the perfect rock for cave-making, and although speleologists have only begun to map the country below ground in recent years, some of them believe that the cave networks are so extensive and so interconnected that it may be possible to wriggle from one end of Mount Lebanon to the other without coming up to the surface. Lebanon has plenty of long cave networks. Jeita Grotto, for example, extends for at least 9 kilometres but hasn't been fully explored and could be much longer. Yammouneh, in the eastern Bekaa is linked to the Afqa Grotto on the other side of Mount Lebanon, and in the past, priests of Astarte, who was venerated at both sites, would cross from one side to the other, underground. Meanwhile in Jounieh, a natural tunnel, enlarged in places by hand, once linked the sacred Phoenician bath - now the St. Georges' Grotto on the corniche - with the temple that previously occupied the grounds of the Greek Catholic basilica up in Harissa.

Two thousand years ago, most of the southern and central Bekaa Valley was wetlands. Then the Romans came and began to drain the valley, turning it into the empire's breadbasket, second only in importance to Egypt. After they left, the draining continued. Today, all that remains lies outside the town of Ammiq. The wetland covers an area of roughly a million square metres and it's a major stop for birds migrating between Europe and Africa. In all, around 260 different species visit annually, mostly in winter months. The wetlands are home to many indigenous threatened species, including the Levant viper, wild boars, hyenas, grey wolves, otters and hedgehogs, as well as, water buffalo, which were brought in to help crop the wetlands sustainably.

The wind can have a powerful effect on the weather. In the winter, when conditions are right, chill winds straight out of Central Asia sweep across Lebanon and can cause temperatures in the Bekaa Valley to drop by ten degrees or more. In the spring, and sometimes again at the end of summer, the opposite happens when a hot wind straight out of the Sahara blows up along the Levantine coast. Known as the Khamsin – Arabic for fifty, the approximate number of days the wind blows after the New Year – it can arrive any time from mid-March to early May and can sometimes register in excess of 40°C. Apart from a temporary spike in temperatures – which can bring a touch of summer to the end of winter – the Khamsin covers the country in a fine layer of sand, and, if it blows hard enough, can even melt the snows on Sannine.

Tripoli was once known as The Fragrant because of the acres of citrus orchards that surrounded it. Beirut too has a perfumed past. Back when most houses and even early apartment buildings had gardens, the city was known for its scented gardens of jasmine, gardenia, basil and frangipani. Of the four, jasmine and basil were the most popular. Jasmine was grown for the hundreds of strongly perfumed flowers it produces, which not only scent the night air but also help keep mosquitoes at bay. Basil, the small-leafed local variety, rather than the large Genoese type, was grown in a pot near the door so that visitors could rub their hands over it before coming into the house, ensuring that however sweaty the day, guests could always arrive sweetly-scented.

2 LIFE

From the proper way to express yourself on Beirut's roads and the literal translations of famous people's names to the biggest families (by size) in the country, Life is all about the people that surround us and the (sometimes) unusual things they do.

AS the popular local phrase killak zo' (rough translation: you are well-mannered /have great taste) suggests, courtesy and good-breeding are integral to Beiruti life. There are, however, exceptions. Like when one is overtaken on the motorway or is required to stop at a red light, for example, when screaming k**s ikhtak, ya akhou sh****ta[1] or the equally unforgettable a**e feek man***ke[2], at the top of your voice, is apparently an acceptable form of (male) social intercourse. Similarly, when running into a friend one hasn't seen for a while, the greeting Yii[3], you're so fat!, Those trousers don't suit you, or, the enquiry, Who cut your hair? – phrased in a way that leaves no doubt that the asker wishes to avoid having his or her hair cut at the same place – all pass for politesse.

1- A common and colourful Lebanese expletive relating to sisters and brothers of whores. The English equivalent, son of a b****, comes close but the Lebanese phrase is far more explicit and indecent.

2- An expletive used on the street between badly-bred men, which references male anatomy and suggests improper behavior at the same time.

3- An informal and entirely acceptable expression of surprise, fear, alarm or disgust (equiv. to ooh, yikes or wow).

Another culturally-specific phrase that reveals a great deal about life in Lebanon is Naeeman. It's what you say to someone after they've had a shower, shaved or cut their hair, and, roughly-speaking expresses the very gentle wish that the post-shower/shave/haircut sensation of freshness lasts as long as possible. Sometimes though, the phrase is the precursor to a sneak attack, in the post-haircut tradition known as the Sahsouh. Practiced by little boys (and some men who haven't fully left their childhood behind), the Sahsouh is the Lebanese equivalent of the American playground gag, the wedgie. Basically, it's a tight slap delivered to the back of the head or the nape of the neck of a person who has just been trimmed. Male-bonding at its very best, its apparently done to take away the chill that follows a haircut. Either that or its done to swat the 20 centimetre mosquito that's about to bite your neck. Anyway, whatever the reason, the Sahsouh is done for your benefit. Definitely not for fun.

Normally though, family honour was enough to keep most children from misbehaving. Generally-speaking, it still is. So much so, that many people spend their lives trying to ensure that they never do anything – or at least never get caught doing anything – that might reflect badly on their relatives. This can be a real problem in Lebanon. The country is so small that no matter where you go, you're bound to run into someone who knows one of your relatives.

If this is an issue for your average Lebanese, imagine how much harder it is for a member of the Zuaitar or el-Merhebi clan. Between them, these two families account for around 45,000 people, or just over 1% of Lebanon's population. Thanks to the Diaspora, some of Lebanon's other big families – the Khourys, Harbs, Kabbaras and the Haddads, for example – have taken that problem to the global level. These lucky individuals not only have to worry about making sure they don't show up the folks back in Beirut, they have to worry about not doing the same in places like London, Paris, Dakar, Sao Paulo and Sydney as well.

Another drawback of being a member of one of Lebanon's biggest families is that while you have relatives all over the place, you don't always know what they look like. Some families, perhaps mindful of the distance that can develop when you have so many relatives that you need an iPhone app to keep track of them all, organize yearly get-togethers. Not only is this a chance to catch up with cousins from Sierra Leone, it's also an opportunity for family members, young and old, to test their face-recognition skills. How helpful they are on this level probably depends how big the gatherings get. Take the Abujaoudeh clan, for example. They've been known to assemble over 5,000 family members at a time, and you have to wonder though if, in this case, a family gathering might not make the problem worse.

Let's say that you don't need to commit Khatifeh (kidnapping) and you even have a date in mind for the wedding but you want to have a romantic weekend away before you get wed. Can you get a room together?
In theory, yes. The Lebanese penal code doesn't say anything about unmarried couples sharing hotel rooms but social mores and Family Law, neither of which tolerate pre-marital sex, sometimes mean that unmarried couples will find it difficult to get a room, especially if one or both of you is Lebanese. Non-Arab guests don't normally have such problems but that's as much due to the general perception that Westerners are wayward and to make a buck, as it is down to the Lebanese impulse to be hospitable.

Though they are marrying later and later in life, marriage is still an important institution for most Lebanese. Not that it's necessarily possible for them to marry whoever they want. For example, the Druze cannot marry outside their communities. However a Muslim man may marry a non-Muslim woman but a Muslim woman may not marry a non-Muslim man. A Maronite man may marry a Muslim woman and she does not have to convert but the children will be Maronite. An Orthodox man may not marry a Muslim woman unless she converts.

So what's a couple to do when they can't get married at home? Go abroad. Mixed and civil marriages performed elsewhere are recognized in Lebanon, so Lebanese who cannot marry without converting or who would rather have a civil ceremony, need to get on a plane. Cyprus is currently the most popular destination because it's close enough to go in the morning, marry in the afternoon and return to Beirut as a couple in the evening. In 2009, just over a thousand couples chose this route and apparently, up from only a couple of hundred a few years earlier. No wonder Cyprus is known as the Island of Love.

IT isn't only one's choice of spouse that is determined by law. Lebanon's different communities are also subject to different ages of consent. Christians and Sunnis can legally marry at 18, if they are men and at 17 if they are women. While no one, in theory, can prevent a marriage from taking place once both partners have reached legal age, Lebanese Shi'ites and Druze can get married at a younger age, if both bride and groom have the permission of their parents or guardians. For the men, this means marriage is possible at 15 (if they are Shi'ite) and 16 (if they are Druze). Druze women can marry at 15 and, while it hardly ever happens any more, Shi'ite girls are legally entitled to marry once they reach 9.

IN the past, children were kept in check by the fear that they might end up stuffed into a sack and carried off, never to be seen again. Just as the Dutch used to frighten their wayward wards with tales of Sinteklaas, the Santa who left the well-behaved presents but carried the naughty ones away, so the villagers of Mount Lebanon used to chill their children with tales of Abou Kees, a travelling merchant who always arrived on a donkey and whose bags – or "kees"[1] – were exactly the right size for carrying away naughty girls and boys.

1- Plural kyaas

IN Lebanon, a person's name tells you their religion and what part of the country they come from. Beyond that, it also tells you a lot about their parents. Just ask Hitler, Mussolini, Malfoufe (Cabbage) or Khasse (Lettuce) – all names given to Lebanese children in recent years.

Nor does the fun end with first names. Some of Lebanon's surnames may be indications of humble origins; Makari (donkey herder), Khoury (priest), Boustani (gardener) and Haddad (blacksmith). Others though, are more revealing of the way one's ancestors were perceived; hence Murr (bitter), Labaki (confused), Karami (generous) and Ghandour (someone who walks with a dance in their step).

It isn't only surnames that are fun to translate. The name of the former Prime Minister Fouad Sanioura, for example, translates as Heart (of the) Beautiful Lady. The current Prime Minister is Happy The Silky, son of Comrade The Silky. Mousbah al-Ahdab, the MP from Tripoli, is Lantern The Hunchback, while Nasser Qandil, the pro-Syrian former MP, is Victorious Jellyfish. Most unfortunate of all? The Mayyar and the Zibara clans. The first translates as "doesn't care" and the second, well let's just say that it suggests a certain male body part that's normally not on view.

B ack when Lebanon was a rural society, weddings could last for up to three days. Today, they're a more condensed affair. This is just as well. Given how much a modern wedding costs, most couples are lucky if they can afford for it to go on for more than a few hours.

Some of the old ways persist though, for even the most contemporary wedding isn't complete without the two Zs: the Zaffeh and the Zaghlouta.

Traditionally, the Zaffeh marked the end of the wedding, the day the groom, escorted by his closest friends, relatives and neighbours, as well as gypsy musicians, dancers and sword players, arrived at the bride's house on horseback to take her away. Sometimes, this still happens today but more usually, it's held as a part of the wedding reception, generally minus the horse. The Zaghlouta? Well, that's either the high-pitched ululating sound of joy made by female relatives as they shower the departing couple with rice and rose petals or it's the high-pitched expression of dismay the groom's mother makes when she gets that bill for the catering.

A bride is considered so lucky that when she arrives at her new home – in the past, her husband's family's house, these days, probably an apartment somewhere in the suburbs – she is said to bring good luck and prosperity with her as she enters her new home. Middle Eastern Christians prefer not to take any chances though, and, to ensure that the marriage gets off to the most auspicious start, they observe a tradition known as Btilzou' el-Ajineh. The bride and groom take a small piece of dough, press a coin into it, make a cross on its surface and then stick it to the wall above the main door. The Ajineh is left in place until it falls off and the longer it stays in place, the more fortunate the bride.

IT is difficult enough in Beirut to sneak home at 3 in the morning without the entire neighbourhood (and then in swift succession, your entire family) knowing every single detail but when it comes to a marriage, the Lebanese like to make sure that anyone who isn't deaf (or possibly dead) will know that the happy day has arrived. The tradition is called Barmit al-Aroos, which translates roughly as the Bride's Tour but could just as easily mean hours of inappropriate and cacophonous noise as the bride-to-be is driven around her neighbourhood, the city and sometimes, it seems, the entire country, in a convoy of cars decked out in acres of gauze and entire hothouses of flowers, with every horn honking in unison. Perhaps the theory is that if the bride wasn't blushing before the Tour, she certainly will be afterwards.

One of the dances performed at the Zaffeh is the Dabkeh. It's similar in some ways to the traditional dances of Greece and Russia, a kind of line dance that involves a lot of swaying, the linking of arms, the stamping of feet and the occasional hop or two. More advanced practitioners get to indulge in the kind of extremely nifty foot-work that takes years of practice to pull off without tripping over.

Exactly how long the people of the Levant have been doing it isn't known for sure, but it's danced in a similar fashion by the Lebanese, the Syrians and the Palestinians.

The story of how the Dabkeh came to be, though, can be told. Apparently back in the days before red roof tiles, when Lebanese houses had flat roofs made of layers of earth and wood, an enterprising man found a way to make repairing his roof much more fun. You see, every couple of years, the roof would have to be remade, as the earth would begin to crack. Tired of doing it all on his own, the man decided to invite his neighbours over to help. He formed them into a line and got them to stamp their feet as they moved along his roof. The new layer of earth was soon firmly fixed in place and, so the story goes, a brand new dance was born.

OF course, some people can't get away from their families even when they move. In most parts of the world, moving to the big city was seen, in part, as a chance to get away from the people you knew back home. Not in Beirut. Here it seems that people are so used to being surrounded by familiar faces that even when they move to the other end of the country, they'd much rather be living next to the people they've known their whole lives.

As a result, Beirut is literally a series of villages. When Borj Hammoud was settled by Armenian refugees fleeing the massacres in Turkey, many chose to live with people from the same village they left behind, naming their new street after their former village. Similarly, as waves of villagers poured into Beirut in search of work, they often settled together. The eastern Beirut neighbourhood of Jeitawi, for example, is full of people from Qartaba. Other neighbourhoods go even further. Zuaitariyye in Fanar, for example, is populated entirely by the Zuaitar clan of the Bekaa Valley.

They say that only two things in life are certain; death and taxes. The Lebanese have a long and storied tradition of avoiding the latter and, out in the villages, an impressive tradition of postponing the former. Take Ali Mohammad Hussein and Hamida Musulmani. Both were farmers, both were born sometime in the 19th Century and both owe their old age to very different causes; Mr. Hussein smoked like a chimney and ate everything, as long as it wasn't processed, while Mrs Musulmani has never smoked and gave up meat when she was younger. Because neither of them have birth certificates – Lebanon had no systematic records system before 1932 – they don't qualify for the official record books but according to the census taken in that year, Ali was born in 1862 and Hamida in 1877. Assuming both birth dates are correct, Ali would have been 136 at the time he passed away in 1998 while Hamida, though frail, is currently 132, which would make her a decade older than the oldest officially recognised person, Jean Calment, who died in 1997 at the age of 122.

However old you were when you died, there was always one thing you could count upon in Lebanon and that was a rousing send off. It didn't matter how well you had lived your life, if you were married with 70 grandchildren or single and childless, whether you had many friends or none at all, a small fee was enough to guarantee that there would be weeping, wailing and yes, even gnashing of the teeth, at your funeral.

The tradition is called Niddebeh and it's as old as the world itself. Niddebeh were (and still are, though there aren't many of them about any more) professional mourners. Usually, though not exclusively, women, the Niddebeh were contracted to help set the mood at a funeral and would stand over the deceased crying, singing laments and sometimes creating a scene by rolling in the dirt and tearing their clothes. In the days before women were allowed to get jobs, becoming a professional mourner was one of the few ways they had to supplement the family income. Most laboured in obscurity but some Niddebeh, who were known for the quality of their laments and their ability to bring tears to mourners eyes, became quite famous and would be contracted to work wakes all over the country.

Weddings are the perfect opportunity for Beirutis to do the three things they like to do best; throw a memorable party, dress to the nines and look around for a possible (and sometimes replacement) spouse. While the event is supposedly all about the bride, there's so much flirting going on between the guests, that the wedding itself sometimes seems like a secondary event. Or an excuse. Perhaps this is why the Lebanese equivalent of throwing the bridal bouquet provides any neglected bride an opportunity to get some revenge. The sign that one of the female guests is next in line to get married? That would be when the bride steps on her foot. By mistake. Of course.

Now the person you want to marry and the person your parents want you to marry are not always one and the same. In England, when a couple wanted to marry but their parents objected, their only choice was to escape to Scotland, to get married in Gretna Green. In Lebanon, the problem is just as difficult but the answer is simpler. It's called Khatifeh. The groom abducts his bride and takes her to the house of a friend or an uncle. Once taken from the family home, social custom requires that the marriage take place, to save face and preserve family honour.

IN some ways, Beirut has historically been a pioneer of womens' rights. It was the first city to have a girls' school in the Ottoman Empire – the American School for Girls, which started up in 1835 and which is better known today as the Lebanese American University (LAU). It was also the first Middle Eastern city to permit women to attend university. When the American University of Beirut opened its doors to women in 1921, Beirut was also the home to courageous women like Nazira Zain al-Din, who was one of the first women in the Middle East to remove her veil.

Unfortunately, that pioneer spirit still does not extend to matters of nationality. Lebanon's nationality law dates back to 1925 – two years before Nazira wrote her treatise on the veil, *Veiling and Unveiling* – and while it allows Lebanese men to confer citizenship to their wives and children after a year of marriage, it does not extend the same privilege to Lebanese women. No matter how long her marriage lasts, a Lebanese woman's spouse and children are forever foreign.

S peaking of children, regardless of how ungrateful, disobedient or difficult a child may become when they grow up, their birth is (usually) a joyous event. Once the baby is delivered and the bowls of meghleh[1] are distributed, the blessing ceremonies begin. Christians perform a baptism, during which the baby is anointed with olive oil and water. Maronites are content to drizzle a little oil on the child's forehead. The Greek Orthodox prefer to coat the child's entire body, for any part that is not anointed is believed to be weak and susceptible to illness.

For Muslims, the blessing is a much simpler affair. The Adhan is whispered into the newborn's ear. A second ceremony, which is known as the tahneek[2], can also be performed but it's becoming less commonplace. This is performed by a pious and virtuous person, usually a religious leader, who chews a piece of date until it becomes a soft paste and then puts the paste in the baby's mouth, giving it protection and a taste, literally, of virtue.

1- A sweet pudding of rice flour spiced with cinnamon and caraway covered with an assortment of nuts, raisins and desiccated coconut, usually made to mark the birth of a baby; and served as an offering to well-wishers. It can also be eaten on ordinary occasions.

2- A birth ritual for newborn babies as practiced by the Prophet Mohammad which involves touching the lips of baby with something sweet, like honey, dates, or sweet juice sometimes by mother or father.

3 HISTORY

From fighting dragons and arguing over who printed the first book to the origin(s) of Beirut's name and which is the oldest city in the world, History is all about the people, places and events that have had a hand in shaping the city's history.

ST. George

may be the patron saint of England, Ethiopia, Barcelona and Moscow but it was here in Beirut that he slew his dragon. Or more accurately, just outside the old city walls. Tradition places the spot in modern-day Qarantina, just north of the old Tripoli road. The chapel that once marked the spot, founded in the 4th Century by St. Helena, is now a mosque called El Khodr. The name means The Green One and refers to one of the teachers of Moses, but it was also an ancient epithet of the saint himself.

The Egyptians call their capital the Mother of the World and the Lebanese call theirs the Lady of the World. Ironically, the Lady is at least 3,000 years older than the Mother.

As befits a lady, Beirut's exact age isn't known. The earliest surviving mention of the city is in a text from the ancient city-state of Ebla, which was written around 2400BC.

That doesn't make Beirut the oldest continually inhabited city in the world. That title is held either by Jericho – although the city was abandoned once in its history and has shifted locations several times – or Byblos, which is slightly younger but has never been abandoned or moved.

Whether Lebanon does have the oldest continually inhabited city in the region or not, it is home to more of the world's oldest continually inhabited cities than any other country.

The Lebanese and the Syrians are always arguing over who was the first to do whatever it was they are arguing over. Take the printed word. The Lebanese say that the first Arabic books printed in the Middle East were produced at the Mar Yuhanna Monastery in Kinchara in 1734. The Syrians counter by saying they were printing Arabic books in Aleppo in 1706.

What neither of them realize is that the first book printed in the Middle East in the Arabic language wasn't even printed in Arabic letters. The Qozhaya Psalter, produced at the Mar Antonius Monastery in the Qadisha Valley in 1610, is a bilingual Syriac-Arabic text, both of which are printed in Syriac.

With the exception of a 400 year stint under the Greeks when it was called Laodicea in Phoenicia and the addition of the prefixes Colonia Julia Augusta Felix in 14BC by Roman Emperor Octavian – in honour both of Berytus' ascension to fully-fledged colony and because his daughter, Julia Augusta, spent her winters here – Beirut has had more or less the same name since it was founded 5,000 years ago. It's been known as Biruta, Ba'urtu, Berytus, Beryte, Berouth, Barut, Birot and Beyrouth and its name is most likely derived from the three-letter Cannanite word for wells, B'rt.

The grace and ease with which modern Beirutis flout their city's many but regularly unobserved laws would have at least two of the city's Roman-era residents turning in their graves. Papinianus and Ulpianus, locally born citizens of the Empire, were Roman jurists and the two greatest professors of law at Beirut's famous law school. One of three schools responsible for writing the Empire's laws – its counterparts were in Rome and Constantinople – the Beirut school was destroyed, along with the rest of the city, by the earthquake of 515AD. Afterwards, it moved briefly to Sidon but failed to flourish in its new home. Today, the only trace it has left behind is in the motto on the city's crest. Berytus Nutrix Legum; Beirut, Mother of Laws.

The name Lebanon has been around for just as long and every single tribe in the region appears to have come up with the same name for it. Like Beirut, which is based on the Cannanite word B'rt, meaning wells, Lebanon is based on the three letters LBN, which in most of the ancient languages in the region meant white. The first surviving mention of Lebanon comes from an Egyptian text, written circa 3,000BC. Transliterated into Assyrian, the Egyptian name, which was used to refer to the highland mountains of Phoenicia, was Labna-a-niI. Another meaning, of the same combination, means to scent/to perfume and comes from the fragrance of the cedars for which Lebanon was once so famous.

Luxor's obelisks (as well as the Elgin Marbles) aren't the only ancient structures to have found new homes abroad. Some of the columns of the Temple of Jupiter in Baalbak have emigrated as well. Even before the earthquake that destroyed much of the temple complex in the 6th Century, bits of Jupiter, which was the largest temple in the Roman world, were being used in new construction. Eight of its 20 metre tall rose granite columns were carted off by Justinian in 440AD to rebuild the Hagia Sophia in Constantinople and, 110 years later, one more was requisitioned by Suleiman the Magnificent to support the dome of his equally magnificent Suleimaniye Mosque.

Before the Mohammad al-Amin Mosque on Martyrs' Square was inaugurated in 2008, Beirut's central mosque was the Omari, on Weygand Street. The site's a classic example of Lebanon's ever-changing religious orientations. In 240AD, Roman Emperor Phillip the Arab built a temple of Jupiter here. The temple became an Orthodox church under the Byzantines and then a Catholic church under the Crusaders, who rededicated the cathedral dedicated to St. John in 1150. According to tradition, one of John's arms is buried there. In 1187, the church was converted into a mosque by Salahdin and then reconverted to a church a decade later when Richard the Lionheart took Beirut. In 1291, after the Mamlukes drove the Crusaders out, the church again became a mosque. And so it remains... for the time being at least.

A long, long time ago, Agenor, King of Tyre had a daughter. She was one of the most beautiful women in the ancient world. So beautiful, that Zeus decided he would have her for his own. The king of Greek gods turned himself into a white bull and waited for her on the seashore. The bull behaved so lovingly that she climbed on his back. Immediately, Zeus took off, carrying her across the sea to Crete. Agenor's daughter never saw her homeland again but she did give her name to her new one; Europa.

Europa's abduction broke her family's heart, so her father Agenor sent her brother out to find her. Prince Cadmus was told not to return until he had his sister with him. He never found her and so, like his sister, Cadmus never saw Tyre again. His gift to the continent his sister named was even greater. Cadmus settled in Greece, founding the city of Thebes, and as he and his companions adapted to their new homeland, they taught the Greeks the Phoenician alphabet, which the Greeks later adapted and extended, creating the first alphabet of their own.

The crumbling old Lebanese homes of Zokak el-Blatt, steadily being replaced these days with soaring tower blocks, are reminders of more than Beirut's architectural heritage. It might not look like much now, but this neighbourhood, the first to be built outside Beirut's city walls, was one of the places where the modern Arab world was born. Ground Zero of the Nahda, the Arab Renaissance that began in the dying decades of Istanbul's 400 year-rule over the region, Zokak al-Blatt was where Ibrahim Yaziji, Hussein Aoueini (both born here), Salim and Butrus al-Bustani, Abdel-Kader al-Kabbani and Khalil Sarkis, lived, wrote and planned for a future free from Ottoman rule. Before it became a neighbourhood, the hill on which Zokak el-Blatt stands was where Beirut's rulers built their winter residences.

Lebanon's reputation as a centre of learning began in the 19th century. That was when the city's – and to all intents and purposes, the region's – first modern Western-style schools were opened. The first schools were clustered in Zokak al-Blatt, which was then the city's newest neighbourhood and the first in the Levant to be paved, thanks to the city's governor Mahmoud Nami Bey. Between 1863, the year the Madrassa al-Wataniyya opened, and 1878, when the first Makassed school opened, Zokak al-Blatt became home to the Sultaniyya, the Uthmaniyya and the Batrakiyya. The Syrian Protestant College, which later became the AUB also began life here in 1866, before moving to the wide-open spaces of Ras Beirut in 1870.

Beirut's linguistic promiscuity has a very long history. Its citizens have spoken at least three languages on a daily basis for hundreds of years. Today, it's the (in)famous mixture of French, English and Arabic known as colloquial Lebanese but three hundred years ago, the mix was different. Turkish was spoken by the city's educated elite; Arabic was spoken by the city's Muslims; and Syriac, though fading, was still spoken by many of the city's Christians. In fact, so many Christians still spoke Syriac that one old Levantine saying, the Arabic equivalent of "when Hell freezes over", was "when Arabic becomes a Christian language".

The Romans turned Heliopolis into the largest religious complex in the Empire, but the people who built the original temple that stood there thousands of years before they came along also had a thing for size. All that's left of their temple, which was dedicated to Ba'al Bekaa, the Lord of the Bekaa, is the Grand Terrace, the massive base on which the Temple of Jupiter is built. The Terrace is made of some pretty big stones. Most are around 10 metres long and weigh around 450 tons, but three of them, called the Trilithium, are double the length and close to 1,000 tons in weight. Quite how the temple builders lifted them into place, like the pyramids in Egypt, no one knows for sure. No one apart from historian Zecharia Sitchin, anyway. According to him, the Grand Terrace was built by aliens in spaceships who used the terrace as a landing spot.

There are castles, or the remains of castles, almost everywhere you look in Lebanon. By the sea, on the top of mountains and guarding strategic passes. Practically every ancient city of importance in Lebanon still has a castle. Sidon has the Sea Castle, Tripoli has St. Gilles, Byblos has the Qalaat. Beirut? Well it had a castle and two free-standing fortified lookout towers too, at least until 1860, when the structures, which had been used by everyone since the Crusaders, were demolished to make way for the expansion of the old port.

The ancient Sumerians invented the sword. The ancient Chinese invented gunpowder. The ancient Lebanese? They invented a colour. But not just any colour. The Phoenicians invented imperial purple, the colour used to dye the robes of royalty around the Mediterranean. The dye was made from murex shellfish, which were left to decompose in vast open-air vats before being boiled. The stench was so powerful, approaching ships could sometimes smell Tyre before they saw it. Because vast numbers of murex were needed to produce the dye – 12,000 or so just to colour the trim of a single robe – Tyrian purple was literally worth its weight in gold.

Some pretty wild claims have been made about the seafaring skills of Lebanon's ancient navigators. We know that the Phoenicans knew the Mediterranean like the back of their hands, that they traded tin in south-western England, sailed the Red Sea and established colonies on the Atlantic coasts of Europe and West Africa. But according to some, they also discovered the Amazon, sailed as far as Rio de Janeiro and built a temple and harbour, now sunken, on the western coast of Australia north of Perth. Herodotus, who is occasionally known as the Father of Lies, also claimed in his *Histories* that the Phoenicians circumnavigated Africa in 600BC, adding that their voyage from the Red Sea around Africa and back to Egypt, took them three years to complete.

IT wasn't only the Romans who made law in Beirut. While cities like Damascus, Baghdad and Cairo have had far more influence in expanding the body of Islamic law, Beirut has played its part too, and, from the 8th century onwards, it was home to the Madhhab, or the school of thought of the Imam al Ouzai. For a time, his rulings became law in Syria, North Africa and Andalucía too. The Imam's religious school used to stand at what is now the Rue Weygand end of the Souk el-Tawile, slightly to the west of the simple sandstone dome that stands there now and which was part of a mausoleum for Beirut's 16th Century Sufi jurist, Ibn Uraq al-Dimashqi.

Although Lady Hester Stanhope, the legendarily eccentric 19th Century British recluse kept camels in Joun to fetch her water from Ain al-Hajar, camels, for the most part, don't figure too heavily in Lebanon's past. The one place you were guaranteed to see them though, was tied up outside the Khan Antoun Bey, down on the docks in Beirut, where they rested on their journeys carrying goods to and from Damascus. It wasn't just trade that travelled by camel to Beirut. Other notable camel-borne arrivals at the port include six massive Assyrian reliefs from Nimrud, Hannah Touma from Tibnin, an émigré to America who arrived after surviving the sinking of the Titanic, and, according to the 1948 Hollywood film *To The Ends of the Earth*, narcotics from Afghanistan.

Over the millennia, Lebanon has passed from conquest to conquest. For its first 2,500 years, the city-states of Phoenicia maintained varying degrees of independence by becoming tributaries to the reigning empires of the time. The first outright conquest, by Persia in 530BC, was followed by successive conquests by Greeks, Romans, Byzantines, Umayyads, Fatimids, Seljuks, Crusaders, Mamlukes, Ottomans and the French. Of them all, the French stayed the shortest time, managing only 22 years and the Romans remained the longest, a total of 461 years, or some 59 years longer than the Ottomans.

AS you blast across the bridge spanning Nahr el-Kalb, halfway between Beirut and Jounieh, spare a thought for the hundreds of thousands before you who died trying. For thousands of years, Nahr el-Kalb was a thorn in the side of the Levant's invading armies. At one time, the river was deep and fast flowing and the cliff on the south side ran all the way down to the sea. The river was the only serious blockage on the otherwise open sweep along the eastern Mediterranean coast. With missiles of all kinds raining down on them from above, soldiers were forced to wade into the sea to get past the gorge, a doubly dangerous prospect in the winter when the river was especially high. Taking the river – named the Wolf River by the Greeks because the wind that blew down the valley in winter storms made a howling noise that could be heard at sea – was such an accomplishment that every army since Nebuchadnezzar's has left a carving in commemoration on the gorge's wall.

S he has died and been reborn a thousand times" is how Lebanese poet Nadia Tueni described the many lives of her hometown. Poetic license aside, Beirut's much quoted reputation as the phoenix city forever rising from its ashes, may be clichéd but it is deserved. In its 5,000 year history, the city has been destroyed entirely or partially a total of seven times by war (Diodorus Tryphon in 140AD and Saladin in 1182), by bombardment (France and Britain in 1840, Italy in 1912 and Israel in 1982 and 2006) and most completely, by natural disaster in 515AD, when the massive earthquake and tsunami that levelled towns and cities all across the eastern Mediterranean, reduced Berytus to rubble, killing 30,000 of its inhabitants.

L ebanon's archaeological wealth doesn't end at its shores. Significant portions of Sidon and Tyre are sunk beneath the sea. In Tyre's case, it's still possible to snorkel over submerged columns and blocks of masonry just off the edge of the existing ruins, but it's possible that the remains may stretch for a kilometre or more into the sea. Elsewhere along the coast, there are sunken remains off Byblos, Batroun and Anfeh, where there may be both a Byzantine and a Crusader port, and Tripoli; while at a spot just south of Jiyye, there's thought to be an entire Roman town off the coast.

IT may not look like much today, more the kind of place you drive through without noticing on your way to or from Tyre, but Sarafand was the Murano of Antiquity. It was here that the art of glass-blowing (and, if Roman historian Pliny is to be believed, possibly even the origin of glass-making, though the jury is out on that one) was discovered in the last decade or so before Christ. Sarafand's modern inhabitants are still making it today and are famous for the delicate turquoise bubble-filled glass they turn into bowls, cups, plates, arguileh bases and even lightbulbs.

MADE IN SARAFAND

The church of Mar Elias Btina in Wata al-Mousseitbe not only contains frescoes dating back to the 11th and 12th Centuries but is built over a small cave, where, according to legend, the prophet Elijah – who is also revered in Islam – took refuge in 900BC. At the time, Elijah was fleeing from Ahab, the wicked king of northern Palestine, and his wife Jezebel, the equally wicked former princess of Sidon, who were determined to make the saint pay for challenging their worship of the god, Ba'al. While he was hiding, Elijah was fed by birds – Ptina in Greek, hence the name of the church – which brought him just enough food each day to allow him to survive long enough to be forgotten.

For an unwieldy beast, the elephant does seem to get around. There are places named after it all over the world; Elephant and Castle in south London, Elephantine Island in southern Egypt and Elephant Butte in New Mexico, to name a few.

East Beirut, a part of the world not normally known for its pachyderms, is in on the act too, as one of its neighbourhoods, Sin el-Fil is Arabic for "the elephant's tooth". Banish images of hidden ivories or caches of tusks though, Sin-el-Fil is likely a corruption of Saint Theophile, patron saint of Antioch, the name held by the neighbourhood during the French Mandate period.

Until 1875, when the British company that was the predecessor of the Beirut Water Company began to supply the city with water from Nahr el-Kalb, the city's residents relied on private and public wells and the Beirut River for their needs. Known in Roman times as the Magoras – and after Beirut Christianized as the Nahr al-Salib, or River of the Cross – water from the Beirut River was diverted into a series of tunnels and pipes that led towards the city on a three-tier aqueduct built by Aurelius in 273AD. The remains of the aqueduct, which was badly destroyed by the 515AD earthquake, still straddle the river near Mansouriye, and the tunnel mouth into which the water was diverted can still be seen high up the southern wall of the gorge.

Beirutis like to have a choice and, when it comes to further education, they're rather spoilt. It may only be home to two million people, but it has 27 registered universities, all but one of them private. They're of varying quality and, like anywhere else, some are more sought after than others. In Beirut, the two big universities are also the two oldest; the American University of Beirut, which was founded in 1866 and the University of Saint Joseph, which was founded nine years later. Both have ties to religious orders, AUB to American Protestant missionaries and USJ to French Jesuits.

F orget New York-style grids, the closest Beirut's anarchic road plan gets to order is in Borj Hammoud. True, Beirut's premier Armenian neighbourhood may look a little jumbled at street-level but it's the only neighbourhood that claims to have been laid out on any kind of grid. This didn't happen because of some far-reaching bit of urban planning but because Borj Hammoud was originally a refugee camp. It was one of the locations where Armenians fleeing the massacres in Turkey in 1915 settled, initially in tents. The tents were laid out in streets, in a grid-like fashion. As the tents became houses, they followed the outlines laid down for the camp and so Borj Hammoud got its grid.

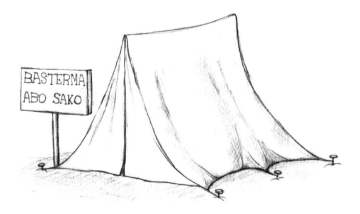

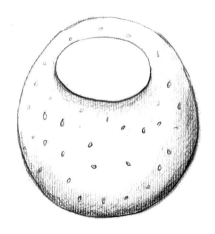

4 FOOD & DRINK

From the medicinal properties of sahlab and the coffee that isn't really a coffee at all to the myriad things you can do with a sheep's testicle, Food and Drink is all about the dishes and the ingredients that make eating in Beirut one of the world's greatest epicurean experiences.

You've just had a lovely meal at a beautiful restaurant in the company of some of your closest friends. The conversation, as always, was sparkling and witty, the flow of thoughts as constant and varied as the flow of the dishes. The evening has been about pleasure, as well as a chance to celebrate your most enduring relationships. Sated, if slightly sleepy, as you sip your après-dinner coffee, you gear up for the final act; the argument over who gets the privilege of paying the bill. All of it. Dinner is not over until one of you has demonstrated both largesse and prowess, by snatching the bill away from your companions. As for the idea of going Dutch, when dining in Lebanon, the only thing that gets shared is the food.

The tomato – which is known as the Banadura in most parts of the Middle East – gave rise to one of the most infamous checkpoint legends of Lebanon's civil war years. Capitalising on the differences in pronunciation – the Lebanese say Ban-a-dura, the Palestinians say Ban-dora – people were sometimes asked to pronounce the word as one way of determining their origin. The irony – if there can be said to be anything remotely ironic about the Banadura test – is that the fruit in question is of entirely foreign origin to begin with. As the Iranians still recognize – they call it a gojeh farangi or a foreign plum – the tomato is an import and wasn't part of the Middle Eastern diet until the 19th Century, when it was introduced to the region by John Barker, the British consul in Aleppo.

With apologies to Khalil Semhat, the farmer from southern Lebanon who dug up an 11.3kg potato in 2008, the world's largest potato, weighing a crushing 37kg, is still the one that was grown in Lanzarote by Manuel Perez in 2004. Chalk that up to the fact that the Spanish have been growing potatoes for much longer than the Lebanese.

Like the tomato, the potato originated in Latin America and was only introduced to the rest of the world after the Spanish conquest in the 15th Century. Before that, the Lebanese fed their appetite for starch with qelqass – the root the Romans called colocasia – which can be boiled, baked or fried but is most frequently (and deliciously) cooked in Beirut with chickpeas and tahini sauce.

Speaking of the ancient Romans, they were fans of another local ingredient; Sahlab. As in the Middle East, they used it to make a hot drink, which was drunk to keep warm in the winter. The Romans believed that sahlab had the power to heat a very, ahem, specific part of the male anatomy – possibly because the classical Greek word orchis, from which the name orchid is derived, means both tuber and testicle – and used it to make aphrodisiacs.

Sahlab is a powder made from the tubers of wild orchids, which are boiled in milk or water, dried and then ground. It was a popular drink in Europe – where it was known as salep or saloop – until coffee became popular in the 17th Century. In Beirut, it's still a winter staple, served sprinkled with cinnamon, and Sahlab powder is used to flavour ice-cream, pastries and is even sprinkled sometimes on Kaake galettes.

Speaking of aphrodisiacs, Sahlab isn't the only food popular in Beirut that's supposed to put lead into your pencil. The Pharaohs believed that Mloukhieh – a plant known in English as Jew's Mallow – did the same thing. Apparently, the more contemporary Egyptians did too. Al-Hakim, the sixth Fatimid Caliph and a central figure in Druze history, banned molokhia on the grounds that it incited debauchery and many traditional Druze still do not eat this otherwise popular dish for just this reason. This probably explains the old Egyptian peasant saying that it's good to keep a bowl of the stuff by your bed on your wedding night. Then there's honey, which not only strengthens your resolve but is also supposed to ensure the night doesn't end too quickly, sea urchins which add vroom to your va-voom and of course bananas, which need no further explanation.

Whether they're round or flat, made of lamb, beef, pumpkin, potato, saffron-tinted rice, red lentils or Kosher bread, stuffed with minced lamb, sheep fat, pine-nuts, spinach, chickpeas, walnuts or cheese, flavoured with Sumac or lemon juice, served fried, baked or raw, cooked in yoghurt, in pomegranate syrup, cherry syrup or in a sauce of tahini and Abu Sfeir, Kibbeh come in dozens of different forms and are eaten everywhere from Beirut to Baghdad. And beyond. They're called Koupes in Cyprus, Koubeiba in Egypt, Kubide in Turkey and Quibe in Brazil.

Like chicken entrails, ashes from a fire and tea-leaves, the grounds left after a person has drunk a cup of coffee can be used to get a glimpse into that person's future. In the Middle East, the tradition is known as Fal and it's probably been practiced since coffee first became a hit with the Sufis in Yemen in the 15th Century. So, your clothes may reveal how you want others to perceive you and your actions may reveal the true nature of your character, but when it comes to revealing your future, it's best to let your coffee cup do all the talking.

IN Lebanon, eating your greens goes way beyond a passion for leaf vegetables like Mloukhieh, spinach, chard and hindbeh (dandelion leaves) or fresh herbs like thyme, rocket, purslane or parsley.

While people almost everywhere else in the world are taught as children that it isn't healthy to eat fruit until it is ripe, unless it is cooked – thanks to their predilection for citrusy foods – the Lebanese take pleasure out of eating many fruits well before they are ready to be plucked.

Grapes (called Hosrom), plums (known as Jararingue) and medlars are all eaten when they're hard and green. Almonds are too, and like green plums, the first ones that appear at the beginning of spring are eaten dipped in salt. Fingertip sized bites, they're eaten whole, fuzzy green casing and all, and the nut within is still a soft jelly. Once the nut hardens, the green casing becomes too tough to eat. At this point, the almond is cracked open, the case thrown away and the soft, creamy nut is eaten fresh.

Finally, there's the pistachio, which is also eaten fresh. Unlike the almond, pistachios can never be eaten whole, their shells are always too tough. Instead, they're served fresh with their purple red skins intact. Peeled and cracked open, the bright green nut within is softer, more delicate and infinitely more delicious than the dried, salted variety that less fortunate people elsewhere in the world know instead.

ON a sweet note, next time you travel to Tripoli and you're looking for an out-of-this-world treat, head to Hajj Nouh's for a plate of Baidaat al Malaikeh or Angel's Testicles. These huge rounds, rolled out of a sugar and rice paste, are flavoured with rosewater and orange blossom and are served stuffed with creamy Kashta and dusted with icing sugar. They may not be actual testicles and are definitely more devilish than angelic, but properly prepared, they do taste heavenly. And if the thought of asking for a plate of balls makes you blush, take heart, the sweet has a second name, so just ask for some Halawet el Shmeyseh instead.

OF course, actual testicles are also eaten. Dipped in seasoned flour, lightly fried and then served with a squeeze of lemon juice and maybe a bit of garlic, Baid Ghanam, lambs testicles, are a popular Lebanese treat.

While it may seem somewhat cruel to deprive a lamb of his testicles, if there is any consolation (albeit posthumous) for the poor lamb it's that once his stones have been removed, there's virtually no other part of him that goes to waste. The spleen (stuffed with garlic and coriander), the brain (turned into omelette, fried or marinated and sliced in a sandwich), the liver (pan-fried or raw), the kidneys (fried and drizzled with lemon juice), the tongue and the bone marrow are all eaten. His flesh is minced and served either raw or cooked as Kibbeh, his intestines are turned into sausage casing and his wool is turned into sweaters. And they say man's best friend is his dog.

IN Lebanon, it might not be good to be a lamb but it isn't much good to be a bird either. Especially not to be the kind of bird that lives in fig groves. For reasons that may remain incomprehensible to anyone who thinks that a bird ought, at least, to have some meat on it, Asafeer, are immensely popular. The popcorn of the feathered world, these birds are thumb-sized and eaten whole, bones and all. Even more meatless than a pigeon – another Lebanese delicacy – the joy of eating Asfour is apparently less the way they taste – mildly figgy, presumably – and more the head popping, spilling hot brains, when you bite into your bird.

Not everything on a local menu requires a willingness to be adventurous. Most Lebanese food is easy on the palate – and delicious to boot – both reasons why it's currently one of the fastest growing global cuisines.

While this is good news for the Lebanese, it probably isn't so welcome for their southern neighbours. For years, restaurants in cities like New York and Amsterdam have been passing off Hommous, Falafel, Kibbeh and Tabbouleh (which is sometimes presented as Kibbutz salad) as a taste of Israel.

This isn't the first experience the Lebanese have of Israel borrowing from them. Previous examples include antiquities from Tyre, water from the Litani River and most of southern Lebanon. But perhaps in this particular case, the Lebanese ought not get overly upset. They say, after all, that imitation is the sincerest form of flattery.

When it comes to weddings, like their counterparts in most other parts of the world, Lebanese brides are usually showered, after successfully tying the knot, with handfuls of rice and rose petals. It's a charming tradition but to an avid eater, it might seem somewhat wasteful. After all, if you turn those rose petals into rose water, boil the rice with some milk, add orange blossom water, pistachios, almonds or maybe some raisins, you have the making of a magnificent pudding, otherwise known as Riz bi Haleeb, rice pudding.

Israel's clumsy attempts at appropriation shouldn't be allowed to overshadow appreciation of the culinary tradition to which the Arab Jewish communities of Iraq, Syria and North Africa are heir.

Some of these dishes are simple twists on Middle Eastern staples. Take Hommous Akhdar, for example, which is made by adding fresh dill to the Hommous or Kibbeh Matfuniya, which uses unleavened Matzoh bread instead of bulgur and meat.

Then there are dishes that are quite different, like kalsonnes Brishtah, a kind of Middle Eastern tortellini, stuffed with cheese or Sofrito, which is chicken sauteed with lemon juice, turmeric and cardamom. Add to this Baid bi Laymoun, a chicken soup made with egg and lemon, Tebit, a slow-cooked meat stew that Iraqi Jews made using a whole chicken stuffed with rice and fast(er) foods, like Sabich, a sandwich made with boiled eggs, fried eggplant, potato, hommous, tahini and mango pickle.

Arab Jews don't only have their own distinctive cuisine, they also have a dish that's named after them; Yahoodi Msafar, which translates as Travelling Jew. A mix of wheat, courgettes and eggplant, it's also known (when eaten by Arab Jews, anyway) as Travelling Muslim.

The Beiruti diner with a penchant for peculiarly named dishes who doesn't fancy a bowlful of Traveller – whatever their religious orientation – can alternatively take a bite of Madame Aisha (white beans in tomato sauce), be the Burner of His Finger (Horra'a Isbaho, a lemony mix of lentils, pasta and croutons) or go for something Thin (M'salwa) a kind of light lentil, rice and onion gruel.

With dinner out of the way, he can tuck into a Lady's Arm (Znoud il Sit, a fried pastry roll stuffed with cream), sample some Bear Droppings (Khiryet el Dibbeh, a sticky semolina cake with almonds) or if layers pastry, cream and nuts appeal, simply Eat and Be Thankful (Kol w' Shkor).

IN Beirut, coffee is always strong, black and bitter. Except when it's white and then it isn't really coffee at all. Kahweh Baida is not the Lebanese version of a café au lait, it's a cup of hot water with a dash of orange blossom water added.

More than just a fragrant way to end a meal, Kahweh Baida is supposed to aid digestion and is sometimes served with candied rose petals. It's also said to calm the nerves, which explains why you'll always find it on the menu at the more expensive restaurants around town.

The last Asiatic lion probably died in Lebanon some time around the turn of the 20th Century but Lebanese lion's milk is still widely available in the country today. Haleeb al-Sbah is one of the alternative names for Arak, a powerful aniseed-flavoured spirit that turns a milky white colour when it is diluted with water. Arak, which comes from the Arabic word for condensation, is produced all over the Mediterranean and the Middle East and is known as Ouzo in Greece and Raki in Turkey. In Iraq, it's made from dates, not grapes, while in Iran, there's a similar spirit known as Aragh-e-Sagi or Dog's Sweat. As to which one is better, well, naturally the Lebanese. Given a choice what would you rather drink, the milk or a lion or the sweat of a dog?

IF some people drink an infusion of orange blossom water to calm their nerves, others drink an infusion of Shilsh el-Zallouh in search of quite a different effect. This hairy root, which grows mostly on Mount Hermon and Kornet el-Sawda, where it is also known as the herb of abundance or Hashisat al-Kattira has become known in recent years as Lebanon's answer to Viagra.

Supposedly powerful enough to give an elderly man back his youth, the Shilsh is most often made into tea. Whether this works is a matter of dispute. While the Shilsh has been proven to stimulate the production of testosterone, the active ingredient is contained in the resin of the root, not in its leaves, so those searching for a little herbal help are probably better off eating it instead.

IN Lebanon, hundreds, perhaps thousands of brides are eaten every day. Don't worry. The brides – or Aroos – in question are not the sacrificial victims of some secret sect that indulges in pre-marital cannibalism, they are in fact, sandwiches. Or, more accurately, rolls. Stuffed with labneh, fresh mint, olives and perhaps a sliver of spring onion, these brides are light and delicious and far less fattening than eating a Lady's Arm (again the English translation of the Lebanese sweet, Znoud il-Sit).

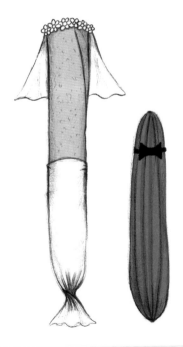

B read is so central to Middle Eastern food that in Egypt, it's simply known as Aish or life.

In Lebanon, bread does not occupy the same central role in life as other things – like having your nails done, going out on a Saturday night or investing in another box of Cuban cigars – but like the Lebanese themselves, Lebanese bread comes in many different varieties.

The two most common are Khibiz Arabi, the light, sweet rounds roughly the size of a basketball and which can be peeled apart and the even larger, slightly sour wholewheat crepe-like version popular in the mountains, which is known as Markouk. Add to this Tannour, a more doughy bread that is rather like the Indian Naan Roti and is prepared in much the same way; Mallet el-Smid, which comes from Tyre and is made with bulgur wheat; nigella seeds and ground pistachios, or Mechtah, which comes from Jibchit and Mouwarraka, a ring-shaped semi-sweet bread made in Amchit, which is stuffed with walnuts and almonds; and then there's Kaak, the crisp sesame studded bread that's often sold (vociferously) by street vendors. Shaped a little like a ladies handbag, Kaak seems to neatly combine the country's twin obsessions; food and fashion.

5 LANDMARKS

From sunken ships and public staircases to the first modern theatre in the Middle East and the bar where Beirut's spies used to go to get plastered, Landmarks is all about the places, long-gone, hidden or still in plain sight, that have made the city what it is today.

Before the Franciscans bought the house on the corner of Goraud and Lebanon streets in 1854 and turned it into the Holy Land convent and church of St. Joseph, it was the home of Maroun Naccache. Naccache was a wealthy 19th Century trader, who travelled extensively in Europe, where he developed a taste for theatre. Deciding that his countrymen deserved to develop a taste for the art too, he turned part of his home into the Middle East's first modern theatre. He staged his first play in 1847. It was an Arabic-language adaptation of Moliere's *The Miser* and probably the first European play to be performed in the region since the end of the Byzantine era. The experience proved so convincing that several members of the audience, thinking the events unfolding before them were real, jumped on to the stage to intervene.

IN the 1920s and 1930s, air travellers to Beirut had to arrive by seaplane, which touched down in St. Georges' Bay in Minet el-Hosn. In 1936, French Mandate authorities began work on Lebanon's first airfield in Bir Hassan. Two years later, the aerodrome opened. It quickly became a favourite stop for European airlines flying to Iran and Asia and, in 1945, it became the base for Lebanon's new national carrier, MEA. Growing air traffic, as well as an expanding city threatened to overwhelm the aerodrome and so a new airport was planned for Khaldeh. When it opened on the 23rd April 1954, Beirut International was the most modern airport in the Middle East.

Martyrs' Square has led a brief but tumultuous life. For most of Beirut's history, it wasn't a square at all and lay outside the city walls. It's been inhabited for millennia though; the Romans built lavish villas here, one of which was recently unearthed on the corner of Weygand Street and in the Byzantine period, a caravanserai stood at what's now the sea-ward end of the square. It first became a square in the 17th Century, when Lebanon's ruler Fakhreddine el-Maani rebuilt the Mamlouk era Borj al-Kashaf tower and added a palace and private gardens, though it remained outside the walls.

In 1772, Beirut was briefly occupied by the Russians, who filled the square with cannons, which is why Martyrs' Square is also sometimes known as Place des Canons. In 1884, the square was made a public garden in honour of Sultan Abdel Hamid II but quickly became a focal point for protests against the Ottoman regime. In 1908, it was renamed Liberty Square and, in 1916, after the Ottomans had twice hung independence activists there, it finally became known as Martyrs' Square.

The name stuck but the gardens were cleared in 1921 to make way for the Beirut Fair. By the late 1950s, Martyrs' Square looked like the iconic image featured on all those pre-war postcards. It didn't last long. The square was levelled during the war and though it's healing again, it still isn't the throbbing heart it used to be.

The battle-damaged statue of Lebanon's martyrs is not the first to grace the square. The original, a sandstone relief by Youssef al-Howayek of two women, one Muslim and one Christian clasping hands over an urn, stood in the square until it was mutilated by a mentally unstable man with an axe in 1948. Today's statue, the work of Italian sculptor Marino Mazzacurati, was erected in the square in 1960 and remained in the city centre throughout the war. In 1996, minus one arm and riddled with bullet-holes, it was taken to the St. Esprit University in Kaslik to be restored but remained there long after work had been finished prompting all kinds of speculation about political decisions preventing its return. It was finally put back on its pedestal in July 2004. Youssef al-Howayek's statue now stands in the grounds of the Sursock Museum.

Nor are all of Lebanon's landmarks on land, either. In its day, the *HMS Victoria* was the lead ship in her class. Then, on 22nd June 1893, she collided with a sister ship during military manoeuvres about six kilometres off Tripoli and swiftly sank, taking 358 men with her, including the commander of what was then known as the British Mediterranean Fleet, Vice-Admiral Tryon. Rediscovered by Lebanese diver Christian Francis in 2004, the *Victoria* is one of only two known vertical wrecks in the world – ironically, the other is another iron-clad battle ship, the Rusalka, which sank in the Gulf of Finland later the same year. The *Victoria* was brand new at the time she sank and went down so quickly, she remained entirely intact. For now, the 68m-long, 10,400-ton ship, which is taller than the Leaning Tower of Pisa, rests sunk to her bow in 30 metres of mud, 150 metres beneath the sea.

Previously known as the home of artistes of a very different kind, today's Saifi Village was the eastern-most extension of the (in)famous red-light district that operated in central Beirut until the end of the civil war. Now one of the city's most expensive neighbourhoods and designated Arts Quarter, Saifi isn't the first of Beirut's new neighbourhoods to be given the title. In 1902, as Beirut was beginning to expand, the Wali of Beirut, Khalil Ibrahim Pasha, decided to make Sanayeh the city's arts district and chose it as the location for the Hamidiyyeh School of Arts and Crafts. It didn't last long. The Hamidiyyeh was turned into a barracks during the French Mandate and afterwards became home to the Ministry of the Interior.

Beirut's first recorded synagogue – in modern time, at least – was built near today's Place de l'Etoile in the mid-19th Century. By the late 1950s, when Beirut's Jewish population reached a peak of 22,000, the city had 17 synagogues, most of them in the old Jewish neighbourhood of Wadi Abou Jamil. Today, only the Maghen Abraham remains. Built in 1925, its construction was financed by Moises Abraham Sassoon, a member of the wealthy Calcuttan trading and banking family. The Sassoons were of Arab origin, originally from Baghdad, grew rich through Britain's opium trade to China and were known at the time as the Rothschilds of Asia. Closed since 1982, when it was (ironically and) badly damaged during the Israeli bombardment and invasion of Beirut, the synagogue is under restoration and is due to reopen in the next few years.

When is a star not a star? When it's a square in central Beirut. Laid out during the French Mandate period, the city's very own Place de l'Etoile was designed to become the focal point of the downtown, an eight-laned version of the star-shaped squares found across Europe. The locations of Beirut's two cathedrals, the Maronite Cathedral of St. George and the Greek Orthodox Cathedral of St. George, however, meant that two of the lanes originally planned to radiate off the square were never built, leaving the star only partially formed.

Time keeping is notoriously fluid in Lebanon, but the city's 19th and 20th Century inhabitants had little excuse for being late. In addition to age-old measures, like the call to prayer and the ringing of church bells at specific times of day, the city had two clock towers. The first, which stands outside the Grand Serail, was built in 1897 by architect Yussef Aftimos and was unveiled on Sultan Abdel Hamid II's birthday. It was the first public Western-style clock tower in Beirut to mark Muslim prayer times and was one of many built around the Empire; there's another in Tripoli, the Ottomans' favourite Levantine city. The second clock tower on Nijmeh Square was a gift to the city in 1933, from wealthy Mexican émigré Michel el-Abed. The sandstone tower is the work of Mardiros Altounian, who also designed the Lebanese Parliament and the National Museum.

When it comes to prominent reminders, the bullet and mortar-riddled skeleton of the former Holiday Inn hotel is difficult to ignore. Just over 27-storeys tall, it dominates Beirut's skyline and will continue to do so at least until the new forest of towers planned for Minet el-Hosn and Wadi Abu Jamil are completed in a couple of years time. Together with the similarly prominent but unfinished Murr Tower just up the road, the Holiday Inn is one of the most notorious of Beirut's wartime buildings still standing. Bitterly contested, for the vantage point it gave snipers, the hotel changed sides several time in a series of bloody battles right at the start of the war in 1975, and, for a while, stood on the original demarcation line between the two halves of the city. And yes, the saucer-shaped extrusion at the top was Beirut's first (and last) revolving restaurant.

Dig almost anywhere in central Beirut and its immediate surroundings and you're almost guaranteed to find gold. Sometimes literally, as with the jewellery routinely unearthed from the Greek and Roman necropolis that stretches beneath most of Gemmayzeh, sometimes in the form of the landmarks of yesteryear. Just beside the synagogue in Wadi Abou Jamil, for example, the remains of the city's hippodrome have been unearthed; while construction of Nijmeh Square in the 1920s and 1930s unearthed the remains of Berytus' Roman forum. Much of that still lies intact under the Assicurazzioni Generali building opposite the glass-clad building that used to be the Banca di Roma, although a few columns were erected in front of the National Museum in Mathaf.

Beirut has always attracted more than its fair share of spies, some less successful at hiding their professional affiliations than others. One of the most notorious in the 1950s and 1960s was Kim Philby, a double, perhaps even triple, agent, with Britain's MI5 and Russia's KGB. A bit of a boozehound, Philby lived in the Normandy Hotel, which used to stand on the opposite side of Minet el-Hosn to the St. Georges. When he wasn't busy spying on his fellow spies – pre-war(s) Beirut was apparently full of them – he was sometimes found keeping an eye on the students at the Middle East Centre for Arabic Studies, an infamous Arabic language school for foreigners up in the mountain village of Shemlan. Opened by the British Foreign Office in 1947, ostensibly to train their own, it quickly became known as the School for Spies, training members of the CIA and MI5 as well as ordinary students. The Centre closed with the civil war but the building still stands. Today, it houses the Help and Hope Institution run by the Social Welfare Institution and is home to 200 mentally handicapped

The twin rock pillars in Raouche are Beirut's most famous natural landmark and one of its most photographed. The grassy promontory in front of the rocks was the first part of the Beirut peninsula to be inhabited back in the 4th Millennium BC. Though it's never been built up, it's still inhabited today, by a small community of fishermen. In the early part of the 20th Century, Raouche was better known for its smugglers and its suicides – the cliff facing the rocks is almost 60 metres in height. These days, Raouche is too public to be an attractive place for the suicidally-inclined, and the only people who still jump off the rocks are local teenagers, who can be seen performing daring Acapulco-style cliff dives off the larger of the two rock pillars in the summer time.

IN the end, the Barakat Building has had a lucky history. Designed by one of early 20th Century Beirut's foremost architects, Youssef Aftimos, and finished in 1934, this golden sandstone building on one corner of the busy intersection in front of Sodeco Square – an old wartime crossing point between East and West Beirut – was one of the first buildings also to use concrete in its construction. Occupied by militias during the war, which used it to control the crossing point, the building's façade was extremely badly damaged and was so riddled with bullet holes that it looked more like Swiss cheese. However, unlike many of its less fortunate (and far less badly-damaged) brethren, the Barakat has not been torn down and is in the process of being turned into Beit Beirut, the city's first museum of urban life.

Thanks to its hilly terrain, Beirut is a city of stairs. In all, there are 120 of them of varying lengths and in varying states of repair and use. Some, like the staircase linking the Corniche and Bliss, are relatively secluded which, together with their proximity to the university, has turned them into an impromptu lover's lane, a whole new twist on Hanafi scholar Imam Shurunbulali's 11th Century oeuvre *The Ascent to Felicity*. The 125-step, 500m long St. Nicholas Stairs, which links Sursock Street to Gouraud Street and is sometimes claimed as the longest public staircase in the Middle East, is known for public displays of a different kind and is regularly used to host outdoor art exhibitions and performances.

Even if very little actually happens inside, its size and prominent location make Beirut's Grand Serail difficult to miss. The city's original serail, or government house, was built in 1884 by Beshara Effendi, the chief engineer of the Vilayet of Beirut, and stood at the northern end of what is now Martyrs' Square. At the time, the building that houses the serail today, up on the bluff overlooking the city centre, was already standing but served as the barracks for the 7th Regiment of the Ottoman Army. It was originally only two storeys tall – the third was added during reconstruction after the civil war – and it was essentially a scaled-down version of Selimiyye barracks in Istanbul. The garden that now extends between the Grand Serail and its neighbour, the Petit Serail, which was built in 1861 as a military hospital, was originally the practice ground where Beirut's Ottoman defenders gathered to train.

Poor old Alfred Sursock, when he leased a 600,000 square metre swathe of Horsh Beirut (which was twice the size of the forest's current area) in 1915 to build a playground for the city's gentry, he had no idea that international geopolitics were about to intervene. He had barely completed the building known today as the Residence des Pins, which was intended as a pleasure palace, when the First World War broke out and it was turned into an Ottoman field hospital instead. In 1918, the French Consul General moved in and it's been the French ambassador's residence ever since. It was from here, on the 1st of September 1920, that General Gouraud declared the creation of Greater Lebanon.

For the first 4,800-odd years of its existence, Beirut was walled. The Phoenicians built the first ones, but across the city, there are still traces of the old Greek, Roman, Persian, Crusader and even Ottoman walls. By the early 19th Century, Beirut was a city of 8,000 crammed into an area about twice the size of Beirut's souks today. Entry was via one of eight gates (Bab in Arabic), several of which gave their names to neighbourhoods that survive today; amongst them Bab Idriss and Bab al-Serail. After millennia of being built and rebuilt, Beirut's walls came down rather abruptly. Caught in a standoff between Britain, Austria, Russia and the Ottomans on one side and the Pasha of Egypt, Muhammad Ali, on the other, Beirut was shelled from the sea by British warships in 1840. Instead of rebuilding, the city's inhabitants decided to tear down the remaining walls instead. Freed from confinement, Beirut began to expand.

Paris has the Eiffel Tower. Sydney has the Opera House. Beirut? Well it has plenty of lovely buildings but nothing, as yet, that is the internationally recognisable face of the city. The Landmark hopes to change all that. Currently rising between ESCWA and the Grand Theatre – a venerable Beiruti institution built in 1925, which hosted everyone from Josephine Baker to the president of the International Feminists Union – the building is the work of French "starchitect" Jean Nouvel and will house a hotel, shopping centre, cinema, health club, offices and luxury apartments. Whether the Landmark will become the face of the city remains to be seen; what is certain is that it will dominate its surroundings; rising 42 storeys high, it will make much of the rest of Beirut look like a toytown.

There's something a little otherworldly about the striking white building – part ziggurat, part Deco skyscraper – that rises above the jumble of buildings behind the USJ campus on Damascus Road, and it isn't just because for many years, it contained a large steel coffin. Designed by Charles Corm, a business tycoon better known today for his poetry and contributions to Phoenicianism, it was completed in 1929 and originally housed Ford's first assembly line in the Middle East. When Corm decided on his 40th birthday to give up his exclusive rights to market Ford's cars in the Middle East – he had 34 outlets around the region by then – the building was turned into the family home and, before it was plundered during the war, there was a 40,000 volume library on the second floor. As for the coffin, well according to urban legend, untrue of course, Corm kept it in a room at the top of the central tower and rested in it when composing his poetry.

Before President Camille Shamaoun decided to move the Presidential Palace up to Baabda, Lebanon's heads of state lived in Kantari in the Ottoman-era sandstone building that belonged to Beshara al-Khoury on the corner of Fakhereddin and Clemenceau. The last President to actually live here was Charles Helou, who was also the first to occupy the palace in Baabda, albeit for only a few months, when it was finished in 1969. After standing empty for years after the war, the building was purchased by Saad al-Hariri and currently houses the offices of his political party, the Future Movement.

With a few notable exceptions – such as the statues of Samir Kassir on Weygand Street and the one of painter Omar Onsi at the foot of the Grand Serail – Beirut's statues tend to commemorate its major political figures; Beshara al-Khoury in Basta, Rafic al-Hariri in Minet el-Hosn and Riad al-Solh, one of Lebanon's founding fathers, on the eponymous square in central Beirut. The work of Italian sculptor Marino Mazzacurati (also responsible for the statue of the Martyrs), Solh's statue was placed here when the square, previously known as Assour Square, was rededicated to him in 1957. It replaced a commemorative marble water fountain, complete with Imperial tughra, dedicated to Sultan Abdel Hamid II that was designed by Youssef Aftimos in 1900. It now stands in the park in Sanayeh.

Not all of Beirut's landmarks are necessarily obvious. Take the Hneine Building, for example. This run-down traditional Lebanese home, which occupies the first block on the right hand side of Rue Abdel Kader just off the Ring Road that slices the neighbourhood of Zokak el-Blatt in two, doesn't look like much from the outside. Scarred by weather, neglect and war, its crumbling sandstone walls, arcades and fragments of stained-glass windows, suggest that once, perhaps not so long ago, it was a beauty. Built in 1800 by a White Russian architect, the Hneine Building has been a private residence, the American Consulate (from 1914-1936); then home to a well-known French doctor, the sister of the writer, Michel Chiha, and for a while in the 1940s, to the blasphemous, scandalous and possibly miraculous, Dr. Dahesh.

Acccoording to popular wisdom, the reason Lebanon doesn't yet have an official war memorial is because there is no consensus on what exactly happened during the country's long years of civil and not-so-civil wars. As a result, Beirut has dozens of small memorials, each of which represent a particular political or sectarian line, but nothing everyone can visit. The closest the country has come to a national monument so far can be found in Yarzeh, outside the beautiful modernist Ministry of Defence. Designed by French artist Armand Fernandez, *Hope for Peace* is a 32-metre tall, 5,000-ton tower of 83 tanks, mortars and other armoured vehicles, sandwiched between thick slabs of concrete. Not to everyone's taste perhaps but well worth a visit, if only to see in which direction the tanks' turrets are pointing.

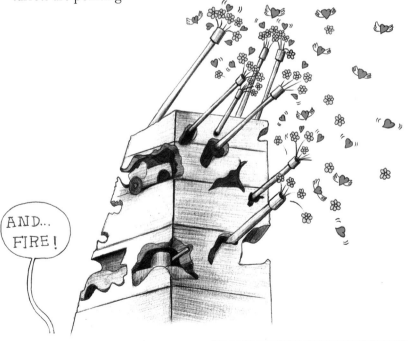

AND... FIRE!

The curious ovoid structure on the platform opposite the Mohammad al-Amin mosque in central Beirut – variously known as the egg or the soap bar – is all that remains of Joseph Phillip Karam's landmark Beirut City Centre project. The egg itself was designed to be a cinema and was supposed to be flanked by two towers. Beneath the platform was a five level shopping centre, which would have been the biggest in the Middle East if the project had been completed. Right on the old Green Line that divided Beirut in two, the centre was destroyed during the war – its solid subterranean structure proved perfect for weapons storage and the cinema was used by snipers. The egg is all that remains, an increasingly rare example of classic 1960s futurism. It's currently used as an impromptu exhibition space and music venue but thanks to the once again prime real estate it occupies, its future is uncertain.

F orget the antagonism between Lebanon's political parties – until the war put an end to one of them – Beirut's greatest rivals were two hotels; the St. Georges and the Phoenicia. Older and more stately, the 1930s St. Georges was favoured by kings, Hollywood stars, multimillionaires and spies, who sipped cocktails on the seafront terrace and swam in the Med. Younger and friskier, the 1950s Phoenicia was favoured by American vice-presidents, Gulf oil men and cabin crew, who swam in the curvilinear pool with a glass wall that gave straight onto the bar. The St. Georges was where Beirut first saw the bikini. The Phoenicia was where it first rode the escalator.

In 1975, the opening salvoes of the war gutted them both. Post-war, the rivalry resumed, albeit more directly, with the owner of the St. Georges, Fadi Khoury, claiming that the new owner of the Phoenicia, Rafic al-Hariri, Prime Minister of Lebanon, didn't want his hotel's old rival to reopen.

6 DIASPORA

From the very earliest emigrants and the
strangest places the Lebanese flag has flown to
the Lebanese connection to Donna Summer,
Diaspora is all about the millions of Lebanese
who have been leaving this country and helping to
enrich others for almost as long as there have been
people living along Lebanon's beautiful coast.

One of the first things that a visitor to Lebanon discovers is that there are many more Lebanese outside of the country than there are in. War, civil unrest, famines, a desire to make a fortune, not to mention plain old curiosity, have driven the Lebanese to almost every corner of the planet, often in their thousands. It's difficult to put a figure on how large the Lebanese Diaspora may be – after all, the first major wave of emigrants dates back to Elissar of Tyre and the founding of Carthage in 814BC, and there have been many major exoduses since then. Estimates that only count emigrants who had or still hold Lebanese nationality, basically those who left during the country's recent wars, place that figure at around a million. Estimates that include second and even third generation Lebanese, whose ancestors may have emigrated a century or more ago, place that figure at between 12 and 14 million, which would make the Lebanese Diaspora larger than those of the Greeks or the Armenians, exceeded in size only by those of India and China.

The Lebanese flag has been flown from some fairly unexpected places. It's made it to the top of Everest, Kilimanjaro, the Matterhorn, Mount McKinley and Aconcagua. The red, white and green has been planted in the ice at the South Pole and flapped wildly in the breeze over the geographic North Pole. But perhaps the most unexpected place of them all is from the top of Number 73, Atta al-Ayoubi Street in Rawda – the address, since 2009, of the first Lebanese embassy in Syria.

Today's Beirutis take great pride in their foreign language skills. Compared to Gibrael el-Sahyouni, a 16th Century native of Ehden, though, even the most competent trilingualist is a slouch. Sent at the tender age of seven to study at the Maronite School in Rome, Sahyouni added Latin, Italian, Turkish, Greek and Hebrew to the Syriac and Arabic he already spoke.

For a while, he taught Oriental languages at the universities of Rome and Venice. Sahyouni's talented tongue caught the attention of Louis XIII, King of France, who arranged for the Ehdenite to move to Paris, where he became the first Lebanese invited to lecture at the Royal Academy and served as the King's official translator.

For all the trouble the Lebanese sometimes have electing their leaders back home, they have no trouble at all producing leaders for other countries. From Elissar and Jezebel, princesses of Tyre in Antiquity, who went on to become the rulers of Carthage and Jerusalem respectively, emigrants of Lebanese origin in more recent times have led Jamaica (Edward Seaga), Ecuador (twice – Jamil Mahuad and Abdala Bucaram), the Dominican Republic (Jacobo Mailuta), Colombia (Julio Turbay), Netherlands Antilles (Emily de Jongh-Elhage) and, in a Vice-Presidential role, Uruguay (Alberto Abdala) as well.

Next time you find yourself wreathed in Cohiba smoke, barely able to taste the mint in your Mojito because the bartender has been overly generous with the rum, remember to raise a toast to Lina Ruz. Cuban by nationality, Lina might possibly have been Lebanese by birth. Records at the time were notoriously unreliable and Lina has been claimed as being of Galician, Mexican and also of Cuban descent.

One lesser-told version of her story is that she was born Angeline Rousse/Ruz in Zehrieh, then a village on the outskirts of Tripoli. Like millions of their compatriots, the Rousse/Ruz family emigrated, first to Mexico and later to Cuba, where Angeline, now known as Lina, found work as a maid and fell in love with her married employer, Angel Castro Argiz. The couple eventually had four children and married; but not before Lina gave birth, in 1926 to a son, Fidel Alejandro Castro, the guerrilla revolutionary and president of Cuba, who like many of his less radical fellow Lebanese, is rarely seen without a cigar between his teeth.

Next time you catch a rerun of *Scooby Doo* – the original 1970s cartoon show, rather than the later remakes or the terrible live action film based on the series – listen out for Kamal Amin Kasem. Better known as Casey Kasem, Kamal Amin is the voice of Scooby's sidekick, Shaggy.(!) He's also a well-known radio host. Together with fellow Lebanese-American, Don Bustany, Kasem was responsible for creating one of the country's most listened-to radio shows, *America's Top 40*.

Who were the first Lebanese and where did they come from? Like almost everything else in Lebanon, that's up for debate – but for now, scholars mostly agree that the first wave of people to settle here were the Canaanites, who originated in the Arabian peninsula eight or nine thousand years ago and gradually migrated north along the Mediterranean coast. Upon discovering our balmy, mountain-fringed shores – which let's face it can only have been an improvement on the desert they had left behind – the Canaanites decided to stay.

So if Lebanon's first inhabitants were migrants themselves, perhaps one day we'll discover that the reason the Lebanese have been emigrating ever since is because it is written in their genes.

Whether the Lebanese have emigration in their genes or not, most people still need a good reason to leave home. Pulling up roots and moving to new, probably completely unfamiliar, land takes gumption.

It's true that Lebanon's very first emigrant, Europa, went entirely against her will and its next famous émigré, Elissar, left in a fit of pique (which didn't stop her from taking half of Tyre with her). Since then, more important considerations have driven the Lebanese to leave; unemployment, instability, famine, occupation and war; and most importantly of all the burning desire to earn enough money to be able to come home, build a big house, buy a fast car and wear very expensive clothes.

Whether Angeline Rousse was really of Lebanese origin or not, she isn't the only famous figure to have been claimed as Lebanese. Neil Armstrong, the first man to walk on the moon, apparently is (or was) too. According to the story, Mr. Armstrong secretly carried a Lebanese flag with him to the moon and planted it just out of camera range, before officially claiming the moon for America. Nor does Armstrong's hidden story end there. Out in the vacuum of space, where sound waves cannot travel, he miraculously heard the sound of the Adhan (the call to prayer) and immediately embraced Islam. Upon returning to earth, Neil grew a beard, developed a fondness for dishdasha and moved, for a couple of years, to Zokak al-Blatt, in central Beirut. Naturally, all this was covered up by the international media but conspiracy theorists can take heart in the fact that at least no one denies that Armstrong did live in Lebanon for a while, even if the Lebanon in question was Lebanon, Ohio and not our delectable slice of the eastern Mediterranean.

IT is possible that Youssef Moussa Chidiac of Miziara was the first Lebanese to officially emigrate to Brazil in 1880. It's also possible that, five years later, Chidiac's neighbour Elias Khoury Younis became the first Arab to settle in Nigeria since the end of the slave trade but sometimes, the claims you find online about other Lebanese emigrants are just plain wrong.

It wasn't a Lebanese landowner and dry-goods trader called Antun Elias Lubbos who in 1808, gave his home in Rio de Janeiro to the then king of Portugal Dom João VI for use as the Imperial residence. It was a Portuguese slave trader with the similar-sounding name of Elias Antonio Lopes instead. American animator William Hanna, partner of Joseph Barbera and co-creator of characters like Yogi Bear, The Jetsons and The Flintstones, might have a surname that sounds Lebanese but his parents were Irish-Americans and not Lebanese. Finally, the rather impressive resume of, Sir Joey Abou Rizk, the 17th Century migrant settler of Catan and later mayor of its capital city, Aiur, is fiction from start to finish, at least outside of the German boardgame in which he is one of the main characters.

The notoriously fluid Lebanese concept of time keeping was something the late Nicholas Hayek obviously didn't inherit from his parents. In other ways though, he was classically Lebanese. Revered as the man who single-handedly saved the Swiss watch industry – this was back in the early 1980s when the avalanche of high-end digital watches from Japan was on the verge of making wind-up watches obsolete – the Man Who Reinvented Time cleverly understood that if Swiss watches were to survive, they needed to be rebranded.

So, as most other Swiss watch sellers were lowering their prices, Hayek raised his. If the Swiss catered to the luxury market, he said, they'd retain their edge.

He was right. Hayek was so successful he decided to found his own brand, Swatch. Today, the Swatch Group owns Blancpain, Omega (the only watch worn on the Moon), Longines, Rado, Tissot, Certina, Mido, Hamilton, Pierre Balmain, Calvin Klein, Flik Flak, Breguet and Lanco. His company is now run by his children, Nicholas and Nayla.

The famous Sir Joey might be a fictional character in a boardgame but the most famous Lebanese emigrant isn't even alive. At least not in its final form. Carried to the four corners of the earth, Lebanese cuisine has not only thrived in places that the Diaspora have settled, but some Lebanese dishes have become part of the diet of non-Lebanese too. In Brazil, the huge numbers of Lebanese descendants – anywhere up to eight million in all – means that dishes like Kibbeh and Sfiha have become an integral part of the average Brazilian diet. Elsewhere, notably in Australia, North America and Europe, snackier foods like Hommous, Babaghanouj, Tabbouleh and stuffed vine-leaves are sold in most large supermarkets; Falafel is proving a popular alternative to the hamburger, and classic Levantine flavours, like Sumac, Za'atar and Hrisseh, have already found new audiences in the world of fusion cuisine.

Ever sat in a crowded restaurant watching the beautiful people walk by and wondered how it is that so many Beirutis live so well, even though most of them are lucky if they earn more than $600 a month?

One of the reasons is that many of them are living on other people's money (or beyond their means). More specifically, they are living on expat Lebanese money. In 2009, Lebanon's generous expatriates sent $7 billion dollars home. That works out to an average of $1750 per person in the country. Not enough to buy a new car, perhaps, but more than enough for a summer's worth of fun-filled Friday nights out on the town.

Carlos Ghosn, the legendary Brazilian-Lebanese president of Renault and Nissan, is probably the only living person of Lebanese descent to have had his life turned into a Japanese comic book. The series, entitled *The True Story of Carlos Ghosn* ran in 2002 and was turned into a book later that year. But Ghosn isn't the only famous Carlos of the Diaspora. Carlos Edde, the president of the Lebanese political party, the National Bloc, was also born in Brazil, while up in Mexico, telecommunications multibillionaire Carlos Slim Helu, overtook Bill Gates in 2010 to become the world's wealthiest man.

Apart from the same first name and Diaspora status, there may be something else the three men have in common. At least if Beirut's rumour-mongers are to be believed. Edde is already actively involved in Lebanese politics but Ghosn, who visits Beirut frequently, is said to have his eye on the Presidency. Slim, who visited Lebanon for the first time in 2010, hasn't made his Lebanese political ambitions known, if he has any in the first place. Still, that hasn't stopped one enterprising person from speaking on his behalf; so whether he wants to be president or not, Mr. Slim now has a Facebook page dedicated to promoting this cause.

Probably the biggest mistake Camil Sabbah – who was born Hassan Kamel Al-Sabbah in Nabatieh in 1895 – ever made was to sign a contract with General Electric. As a result, the 43 patents held in his name, which include applications later used in television transmission and power generation as well as the invention, three years before his untimely death in a car crash in 1933, of the world's first solar cell, were automatically the property of his employer. Sabbah's reward for making GE enormous sums of money? Obscurity and the princely sum of one US dollar per patent received.

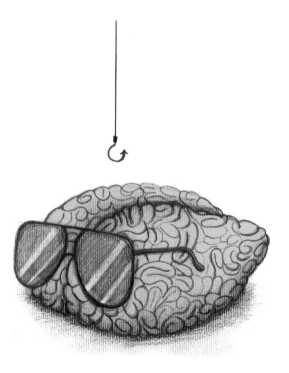

L ater Lebanese inventors were more successful than poor old Kamel. Charles Elachi, the director of the Jet Propulsion Laboratory in Pasadena, California owns patents on several devices currently used in space exploration by NASA. The late Michael DeBakey (née Debaghi), a gifted Lebanese-American heart surgeon, invented a pump which made open-heart surgery possible; discovered that Dacron could be used to replace faulty arteries; pioneered the practice of remote surgery, known as telemedicine; and was working, until his death, on the creation of a self-contained, miniaturized artificial heart.

Perhaps most successful of all though, is Paul Orfalea, the eccentric son of two Lebanese garment sellers in Los Angeles. In 1970, he had the bright idea of providing university students in Santa Barbara in California with access to cheap photocopying services and later, to sell stationery door-to-door in the university dorms. Business soon grew and Orfalea began to open copy shops all over the US and eventually abroad; and in honour of his famously curly red hair, he named his company Kinkos.

There is almost nowhere on earth the Lebanese haven't been and, were it not for the terrible tragedy that befell the Space Shuttle Challenger in 1986, they would have made it into space as well. One of the astronauts who lost her life when the Shuttle exploded shortly after take-off was Sharon Christa McAuliffe (née Corrigan), a school teacher from Boston in Massachusetts. Like many Americans, McAuliffe was of mixed descent. Her mother, Grace Mary George was half-Lebanese and the niece of the historian, Philip Khuri Hitti, who taught Middle Eastern studies at the American universities of Princeton and Harvard.

Since it was first published in 1923, Gibran Khalil Gibran's *The Prophet* has never been out of print and is believed to have sold in excess of 100 million copies, which places Gibran third, behind Shakespeare and Lao-Tzu, as one of the most widely-read poets in the English language.

Gibran isn't the only author of Lebanese descent who found global fame. In 1971, a comedy script-writer by the name of William Peter Blatty – the son of Lebanese immigrants Mary Mouakad and Peter Blatty – turned a story he had heard at Georgetown University into a novel that remained on the New York Times bestseller list for 57 weeks, for 17 of them as the number one bestseller. Two years later, his novel, *The Exorcist*, was turned into a film that has grossed over half a billion dollars since it was released.

Lebanon has long had a knack for turning out talented vocalists. From Fairouz and Sabah to Nancy, Haifa and Nawal, the country has produced more than its share of famous singers. The Diaspora hasn't done too badly either. Paul Anka, Paul Jabara (who also wrote *Last Dance* for Donna Summer and *It's Raining Men* for the Weather Girls), Karl Wolf, Mika and Shakira are all of Lebanese descent, as is Gabriel Yared, a composer rather than a singer, who won both an Oscar and a Grammy for his soundtrack for Anthony Minghella's 1996 film adaptation of Michael Ondaatje's *The English Patient.*

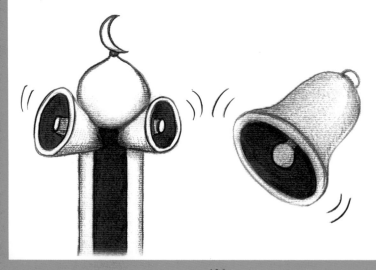

7 RELIGION & SOCIETY

From the burial place of prophets and the
country's first Ethiopian immigrants to the
precise number of officially recognised sects
in the country (which you think you know but
I'm betting you don't), Religion and Society is
all about the people and the beliefs that make
Lebanon such a fascinating place to live.

Anyone who thinks Christmas comes but once a year has obviously never been to Lebanon.

Christians here follow three different calendars; the Gregorian, the Julian and the Armenian. The Armenian and the Julian calendar are essentially the same, except when it comes to Christmas but the Gregorian and the Julian calendar are currently out of synch by 13 days.

So although everyone celebrates Christmas on their equivalent of the 25th of December, when viewed through the Gregorian calendar, Lebanon's Catholics and Protestants celebrate on December 25th, the Armenians on January 6th and the Orthodox on January 7th.

Nor are Lebanon's Muslims left out of the doubling-up fun. With Islam's two main branches, the Sunnites and the Shi'ites, enjoying different interpretations of the lunar calendars, the dates of festivals like Eid al-Adha don't always coincide either, although the difference is less dramatic, generally only a matter of a day.

CAN'T UNDERSTAND WHY DO WE HAVE TO GO 3 TIMES EVERY YEAR TO LEBANON!

C hristians who were Druze. Shi'ites who were Sunnites. Descendants of the family of the Prophet Mohammad – Qoreish – who are Greek Orthodox today. Despite the best efforts of the country's assorted religious authorities to ensure their flocks do not stray, Lebanon has a tradition of religious flexiblility, especially when compared to its neighbours. Take Ahmad Fares Chidiyaq, for example. He was one of the founding fathers of the Nahda, the Arab cultural and political awakening that swept the region in the last decades of the Ottoman era. Born Maronite, Chidiyaq first became a Protestant and then later in life, a Muslim, and only missed out on belonging at one time or another to all of Lebanon's main religions by not having been born Druze.

N oah and Seth aren't the only descendents of prophets buried in the Bekaa. Just on the edge of Baalbek, the unmistakably Iranian outlines of the modern blue and white tiled shrine to Sayida Khawla is built over the burial place of one of the daughters of Hussein, the grandson of the prophet Mohammad. Captured along with the surviving members of her family after the battle of Karbala in 680AD, where her father was famously martyred, Khawla died in Baalbek en route to Damascus. She was buried on the spot by her brother Zayn al-Abideen, who marked his sister's grave by planting the tree that still grows in the middle of the shrine today.

Stop your average Beiruti in the street today and ask him what comes to mind when he hears the word Ethiopian and he's likely to say maid. This is a shame. Not just because of the prejudice it reveals, but because it completely overlooks the fact that Ethiopians have been part of Lebanese life since at least the 11th Century and possibly centuries longer.

Those first Ethiopians also came to Lebanon to work, although in their case, the work in question was God's, not Madame's. No doubt attracted by the famous monasteries in the Qadisha Valley, they came as pilgrims. Some became hermits, dedicating their lives to quiet contemplation in the valley's caves. Others joined local religious orders and, for centuries, there was a community of Ethiopian monks resident in Ehden.

In 1488, that residency came to an end. Owing to religious differences between the Ethiopians and their Maronite neighbours, the monks were expelled from Ehden. They didn't travel far though, finding refuge at the monastery of Mar Assia in the Qannoubine Valley, and remaining, as the traces of their distinctive Ethiopic script decoration on the frescoes of the monastery's walls attest, until well into the 18th Century.

IN the village of Karak Nuh, a kilometre north of Zahleh, there's a roadside mosque that contains the tomb of Noah. Yes, that Noah. The one with the ark. 42 meters long and almost 3 meters wide, Noah was clearly a large man, apparently so large that he had to be buried with his knees bent. According to another story though, Noah could straddle the Bekaa valley, standing with one leg on Mount Lebanon and the other on the Anti-Lebanon, and his tomb only contains one of his legs. Bent double, of course.

If you're wondering how Noah got to the Bekaa from Mt. Ararat – the mountain on the Turkish-Armenian border where tradition has it that his ark landed – well, he didn't. That's because Noah's ark didn't land on Ararat. At least not according to the inhabitants of Tibnin, who insist it landed near their village. Nor is Noah the first member of his family to be buried in the Bekaa. His great-great grandfather's great great-grandfather, Seth, who is the third son of Adam and Eve, is buried in an even longer tomb in the village mosque in Nabi Shith.

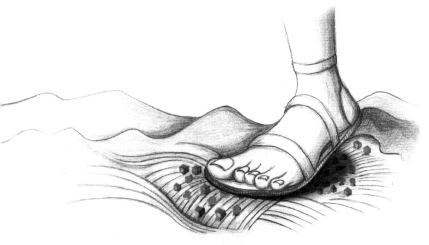

IN Lebanon, it isn't only Christians who go to church. Dotted around the country, there are Christian places of worship which also attract Muslim and Druze visitors. These include the churches of St. Sharbel in Annaya, St. Hardini in Kfifan, St. Rafqa in Jrabta and the grotto of St. George in Jounieh.

The pan-sectarian popularity of these places is because they are believed to be places of healing and, like Lourdes or Medugorje, they are associated with miraculous events. St. Hardini, for example, is visited by couples having trouble conceiving. St. Rafqa is visited by those seeking a cure for cancer and, at the grotto of St. George, the pool of water in front is said to cure children who aren't growing properly – probably, according to Lebanese superstition, because an adult stepped over them and so stunted their growth. Of the four, St. Sharbel, is the real all-rounder, curing disease, paralysis and granting children to the infertile.

Lebanon doesn't get a mention in the Koran but the Bible can't get enough of the place. Between the Old and New Testaments, Lebanon appears 64 times in the King James version. Sometimes, the name refers to a country, sometimes to the mountains, sometimes to a valley and sometimes simply to the beauty of its nature. A number of other Lebanese locations are also mentioned, amongst them Tyre (which appears 57 times), Sidon (50 times), Jbeil (as Gebal - 5 times), Mt. Hermon (Jabal al-Sheikh - 15 times) and finally Baal Gad, which may be modern-day Hasbaya.

When is a Druze not a Druze? Pretty much all of the time and no, this is not some veiled reference to the sect's practice of taquiyyah, the religiously sanctioned tradition of dissimulation to avoid persecution.

Much like Hindu – a meaningless English invention no Hindu would use to describe themselves in their own language – Druze may be the name by which the followers of this sect are universally known outside their community but, when referring to themselves, they prefer to be called Muwahhiddun (Monotheists) or Ahl al-Tawhid (People of Unity).

That's because, despite its ubiquity, the term Druze is offensive. While there are different explanations for how the sect got this name – including claims that the word Druze is derived from the Persian word for Bliss or the Arabic for those who study – the likeliest explanation is that it's a derivation of the name of one of the sect's first leaders, Muhammad bin Ismail al-Darazi. Wondering why that might be offensive? Simple. Al-Darazi was a renegade preacher whose teachings were at odds with the faith's tenets, for which he was eventually executed. So in a sense, calling the Muwahhiddun Druze is the religious equivalent of calling a Stalinist a Trotskyite.

When it comes to clashes of civilisations, Lebanon is often taken as the textbook example. What is overlooked by this dramatic but simplistic reading of the country's history are the ties that bind its people together, the shared traditions and the long periods of co-existence during which the very sects supposedly unable to live together have not only co-existed but also celebrated each others' existence.

Not that long ago, pilgrims departing on the Hajj were blessed by both Muslim and Christian religious figures and Muslim notables often attended major church ceremonies. Until the 1970s, for example, the upper balcony of the St. Georges' Orthodox Cathedral in Tripoli was reserved for Muslims wishing to watch the Easter proceedings.

Although it has taken a bit of a beating in recent decades, that spirit of mutual celebration and peaceful coexistence has not died. Christians attend iftar dinners. Muslims put up Christmas decorations. Messages of congratulations are sent between the sects in celebration of each others' religious festivals. Even during the war, when sectarian sentiments were at their highest, many Beirutis refused to recognise the enforced division of their city by finding reasons to cross from east to west and vice-versa, despite the danger. Simple acts, perhaps, but in many ways, far more telling than the country's bloodier periods.

L ebanon's Jewish population may have been small, especially when compared to the ancient communities that existed in countries like Iraq, Egypt and Tunisia, but it was the only Jewish community in an Arab country that increased in size after Israel declared itself a state in 1948.

As the political fallout from the expulsion of the Palestinians began to make life difficult for Arab Jews in their home countries, some chose to move to Lebanon, which continued to make them welcome. By the 1950s, the community had reached its historic high of around 22,000. The expansion was temporary. At about the time of the 1958 civil unrest, Lebanese Jews began to leave, a process that gathered steam through the 1960s. By the start of the 1975 civil war, the community was down to a couple of thousand, most of whom left to avoid the fighting. Today, a community of around a hundred remain, while another two thousand or so visit on a regular basis.

A sh Wednesday, Spy Wednesday, Drum Wednesday, Holy Wednesday, Great Wednesday, the Wednesday before Easter has many different names and several different meanings. To all Christians, it marks the day that Judas Iscariot agreed to betray Jesus to the Sanhedrin for those 30 silver pieces. To Orthodox Christians, it's also the day that Mary Magdalene anointed Jesus before his crucifixion. To the Maronites, who call it Job's Wednesday, after the prophet supposedly buried in Niha, it marks the start of summer and is the one day that you should not sweep your house because if you do, it's sure to be invaded by armies of ants.

Ever thought there might be a bit more to the warmth of the ties between Iran and Lebanon's Shi'ites than Hezbollah? You'd be right. It's thanks to charismatic preachers from Jabal Amel, that Iran became Shi'ite in the first place.

A majority Sunni nation until the 16th Century, the Iranians converted to Shi'ism for a variety of reasons, but partially as a way to differentiate themselves from the major Islamic powers of the time. To speed the process along, Iran's Safavid rulers brought Arab Shi'ite preachers in to spread the word. In fact, it's safe to say that without Lebanon, there may never have been an Ayatollah Khomeini at all.

The Jabal Amel preachers proved especially persuasive and quickly became favourites of the state. One of them, Sheikh Lotfallah, who was originally from Mays al Jabal, was so beloved that Shah Abbas I built a religious school in his honour. It's still there today, just opposite the Ali Qapu Palace in Isfahan, and its intricate patterned dome is one of the most photographed and widely-recognised in the world.

So, how many sects are there in Lebanon? For all their religious diversity, most Lebanese don't know the actual number of officially recognised sects in their country. The standard answer is 17, as most people forget to include Lebanese Jews, although some do and answer with 18. Both are actually wrong. The real answer is 19; 12 Christian denominations, 5 Muslim denominations and the Jews. The last officially recognised sect? Aetheists, of course.

I T might sound like a case of anything you can do, I can do better but Egypt isn't the only country in the Middle East that has mummies. Lebanon has them, naturally-preserved and Maronite to boot. The two most famous are both religious men, the 18th century Patriarch Youssef Tyan, who died in Qannoubine in 1808 and whose body was rediscovered over a century later, and Lebanon's newest saint, Estephan Nehmeh, who lies in a glass coffin in Kfifan. There are secular Maronites, too, like the mummy of Lebanese nationalist and freedom fighter, Youssef Bey Karam, who lies in state in the St. Georges' Church in Ehden. The country's oldest mummified remains, those of eight Maronite villagers, who took refuge from the Mamluke-Crusader-fighting in a cave in Qadisha in 1283AD, are locked safely away in storage at the National Museum.

Tell the average believer that they know nothing about their religion and you're likely to start a fight. Tell the average Druze they known nothing about their religion – assuming you know anything about it yourself, of course – and they'll probably agree.

The Druze divided themselves into two categories; Jahhal and Uqqal. The Jahhal (the ignorant) form the majority of the community. They know only the basics of their faith, are not allowed to read Druze holy books and are not permitted to attend religious meetings. The Uqqal (the knowledgeable) are a much smaller group. They learn the details of the faith, read the holy texts and attend religious gatherings. Uqqal can be either male or female and are recognised by their distinctive dress; shaved heads, white caps, large moustaches and black, baggy sherwal pants for the men, modest black dress and a translucent white veil called a mandal for the women. The best of the Uqqal can choose to become Ajawid, the group from which the community's religious leaders are taken.

The Druze aren't the only of Lebanon's religious communities with a talent for keeping their beliefs to themselves. The Alawites, who mostly live in and around Tripoli as well as in the currently-occupied border town of Ghajjar, present a similar unknown. Ostensibly, Shi'ites – the community has been recognised as such by several notable Shi'ite scholars, including the long-missing Imam, Musa Sadr – no one outside the community knows what their beliefs are for sure. It's well-known that the Alawis observe some Christian festivals, including Christmas, Easter and Palm Sunday, though in their own, distinctive way, and that bread and wine are used in their religious ceremonies. Beyond that, it's claimed the Alawis believe in a kind of trinity and believe that the Shari'a contains a hidden meaning that only a few have ever understood.

Why the secrecy? Like many of the Middle East's religious minorities, the Alawites have not always had a happy history and have learned the hard way that, sometimes, discretion is the better part of valour.

Over the centuries, the mountains of Lebanon have developed a reputation as a place of refuge for groups of people who, depending on their personal allegiances, are either heretics or true believers. But Lebanon hasn't only attracted heretics; it's given birth to some notable ones too, amongst them, Sheikh Adi ibn Musafir al-Umawi, a descendent of the 4th Ummayad Caliph.

There was nothing *adi,* or regular, about this sheikh though. Born in the Bekaa, the Sheikh is one of the most important figures in the Yezidi faith and is believed by his majority Kurdish followers to be an incarnation of the Tawus Melek, the chief angel of heaven, who was charged by God with the care of the world. Sheikh Adi, born a man, became an avatar of the Tawus and is believed to watch over the world by his side; and his tomb in Lalish, a village north of Mosul, is the site of an annual six-day pilgrimage every year.

Many of the major figures of the Old and New Testament are shared by Christians and Muslims alike, even if there is disagreement between the two religions as to the roles they played. Blessed in both faiths is Mary, virgin mother of Jesus. In 2010, in recognition of the shared reverence both religions have for Mary, Lebanon declared the creation of a new religious holiday. From here on, March 25th, which is already celebrated by Christians as the Feast of the Annunciation, the day Mary was visited by Gabriel and told she was to be the mother of Jesus, will also become the country's – and the world's – first shared Christian-Muslim holiday.

New to Lebanon and wondering what religion the person you're talking to believes in but you're too shy to ask? Here are two handy tricks for getting a rough idea. The first is called the Qaf Test. In Lebanese dialect, the letter q – which is part of common words like manqoushe (a kind of Lebanese pizza) and qoul (speak) – is normally silent, becoming a kind of glottal stop. Except, that is, amongst the Druze, who qaf away in all the letter's glory.

The second, which you could call the Praise Be test is based on the different ways Lebanon's Christians and Muslims say the phrase Al Hamdulillah – Praise Be to God. Muslims will savour the word in its full Arabic glory, pronouncing each syllable clearly. For their part, Christians tend to abbreviate slightly, turning the word into Lham-dillah instead of Al Ham-du-lil-lah.

S heikh Adi is lucky he was born so long ago. Get accused of aspirations to godhood in modern Lebanon and things don't go quite as well. Take Salim Moussa Achi, the man better known in Beirut as Dr. Dahesh.

A writer and a humanist, Dahesh was also a miracle worker. Amongst other marvels, the doctor was supposed to be able to heal disease and to appear in many places at the same time. While this didn't make Lebanon's clergy terribly happy, it wasn't until the doctor began to claim that he was a prophet that he finally pushed one button too many. In 1944, two years after he caused a scandal by declaring that the salvation of mankind lay, amongst other things, in the uniting of all religions, Dahesh was stripped of his nationality and forced into exile.

Three years later, photographs began to circulate in Beirut of the doctor's bullet-ridden corpse, followed by press reports that he had been executed by a firing squad in Azerbaijan. Nothing if not a consummate showman, the doctor apparently saved his greatest miracle for last, for in 1953, after lobbying by several of his more influential devotees got his nationality reinstated, the doctor had a second coming and returned to Beirut with nary a bullet-hole in sight.

8 HEALTH & BEAUTY

From the second most popular form of plastic surgery and the first women physicians to your teta's bon marché way of losing excess weight and the classical origins of Lebanon's obsession with loveliness, Health and Beauty is all about the lengths to which Beirutis will go to keep looking good.

IN Beirut, looking good is more than a past time; it's practically a patriotic duty, and the emphasis is always on looking smart. The unironed look is taken as evidence that you are lazy, rather than maybe laid-back and, while it is easy to appear under-dressed, it is almost impossible to be over-dressed. This is not the kind of city that goes in for Casual Fridays and does not believe the answer to bad hair is a baseball cap. Even a quick trip to the corner store means dressing up, not in anything designer (unless you insist) but certainly no tracksuits either. Life may be a stage, but Beirut is its catwalk.

You've come a long way, baby. When they do decide to get a bit of work done, lucky Beirutis are spoiled for choice. From only six plastic surgeons in 1965, Lebanon now has seventy and a further hundred or so who aren't licensed. That's one registered plastic surgeon for every 57,387 inhabitants; one for every 23,629 inhabitants if you include those that are off the books.

Women are the core clientele but men too are developing an appreciation for a good cut. At the moment, they account for 30% of all the surgeries performed in the Beirut business, but the figure is rising. Foreigners too are flooding in, attracted by Beirut's lower costs, skilled surgeons and the prospect of getting a nip or tuck away from the eyes of family or friends.

The Syrians have an intense love affair with tinted windows on cars. The Lebanese have an equally intense love of tinted glass too, but they prefer to wear theirs on their faces. On the streets, on the beach, in the car, in cafés, restaurants and even, surreally, in cinemas and nightclubs, the Lebanese appreciation for sunglasses is difficult to miss and clearly, some people find it difficult to take them off. Although it's disconcerting to hold a conversation with someone wearing a pair, the current craze for 1970s porn sunglasses – mirrored Aviators and their ilk – does at least mean that even if you can't see the person you are talking to, you can at least use their lenses to adjust your hair and check your teeth for sesame seeds.

Unfortunately, Lebanon's plastic surgeons are still required to deal with injuries resulting from the country's periodic bouts of violence but these days most of them make their living from elective surgeries. Liposuction, breast augmentation, face-lifts, butt lifts, pec implants, permanent eyeliner, permanent lipliner, tummy tucks, hair removal, hair implants. There's almost no part of the body they can't suck, tuck, snip, pluck or stuff.

Still, the most popular appendage of all is the nose. The combination of Levantine genetics and the somewhat peculiar belief that noses look cuter when they've been trimmed out of existence means that Rhinoplasty is the number one surgery in Lebanon, for both men and women. Fairouz blazed the way back in the 1970s, when she had her nose visibly altered and these days there's barely a pop star that hasn't followed suit. Nancy Ajram, Amal Hijazi, Mai Hariri, Wael Kfoury. And of course, Haifa Wehbe, although she claims she's only had a retouch. To her nose, anyway.

When it comes to looking their best, many Beirutis aren't shy of going under the knife. In fact, in some parts of the city and amongst certain social circles, a prominent bandage or a plaster – proof that one has been improved – is practically a badge of honour. Hospital white does look great against a tan, which also helps hide the bruises (in case you needed telling) but it can be hell to find a handbag to match. One thing Lebanon has no shortage of is couturiers, so maybe it's only a matter of time before one of them comes out with a line of designer medical supplies. Then your most pressing choice will be whether to match the Rabih Keyrouz gauze or the Elie Saab bandage with your outfit.

E xactly how many plastic surgeries get performed in Beirut every year is a matter of debate. Certainly the figure must be in the thousands, perhaps even the hundreds of thousands. A couple of years back, one newspaper report claimed that 1.5 million plastic surgeries were done every year. And that was without including things like Botox.

It's an impressive sounding figure but is it realistic? If there are only 70 (licensed) plastic surgeons in Beirut – okay, 170, if you include the unlicensed ones – that would mean that each and every one of Lebanon's plastic surgeons, licensed or otherwise, are performing 24 surgeries a day, seven days a week, 365 days a year.

Unless they're robots or else plastic surgeries are also being done at home on the kitchen table, 1.5 million seems like a stretch. Still, 300 Greeks managed to hold back the entire Persian army for a couple of days back in 480BC, so maybe Lebanon's plastic surgeons are really superheroes in disguise.

Dubious statistics aside, the story kicked off a firestorm amongst Beirut's chatterati, many of whom took it as further proof that contemporary Lebanese society is shallow and fickle.

What most of the moralising over the merits of plastic surgery overlooked is that the speciality was originally developed to help correct physical trauma resulting from war. Although it's been around since the 3rd millennium BC (the ancient Egyptians performed skin grafts and the early Indians could repair lips, ears and noses), the growth years of plastic surgery were during the First and Second World Wars.

Lebanon is a case in point. The country's plastic surgery industry grew out of the demand created by the civil war. But even then, it wasn't only the unfortunate victims of Lebanon's wars that were operated upon.

Bekaa Valley's military commanders – amongst them Imad Mughniyeh, who apparently had so many surgeries that his own relatives couldn't recognise him – relied on Beirut's plastic surgeons to help keep them one step ahead of their pursuers.

IT isn't only women who come in asking for Angelina's lips, Nancy's nose or Haifa's boobs. Sexual reassignment surgery – a sex change in common parlance – is a long and costly procedure, but Beirut, in terms of the numbers of operations performed each year, is second only to Tehran.

That's right. Tehran. After the late Ayatollah Khomeini issued a ruling permitting the operation, sexual reassignment surgery has been used by the Iranian state as a way to pressure gay and lesbian Iranians, who are told to undergo surgery to be given the gender appropriate to their sexual orientation or face the legal consequences.

In Beirut, coercion is not usually a factor. The skill of the city's surgeons, the quality of its hospitals and the perception, warranted or not, that Beirut is a liberal oasis when it comes to sexuality, has made the city the prime destination for Arabs seeking the operation and a popular place for post-operative transsexuals to live afterwards.

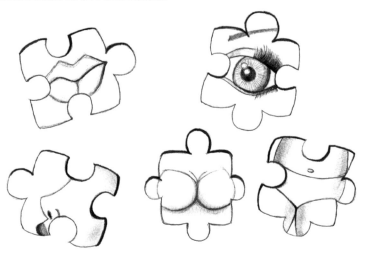

However generous they may have been sharing their own bodies, most Lebanese men (and their parents) still expect the women they marry to have given theirs to no one else.

True, no one expects the post-nuptial bed sheets to be hung outside the bedroom door after the couple's first night together, but in 21st Century Lebanon, women who do not provide their husbands with visible proof that they were previously intact risk putting a strain on their marriage, or worse, the prospect of immediate divorce.

That's why the second most popular plastic surgery in Lebanon is the hymenoplasty, a procedure that can restore the semblance of a woman's virginity. Costing anywhere between $300 and $3,000, hymenoplasties are usually performed off the books, to protect the woman's reputation. Most of the time, the woman's husband-to-be doesn't know but sometimes it's the husband who asks the surgeon to perform the operation on his future wife. The Born Again Virgin is testimony to the huge contradiction in the heart of Middle Eastern, and especially Lebanese, sexual mores; outwardly permissive, inwardly conservative.

The Lebanese obsession with physical beauty earns the country somewhat self-righteous criticism from the more conservative parts of the region but to anyone familiar with the country's ancient history, it comes as no surprise.

The ancient Greeks may have given the world Helen and the ancient Egyptians, Cleopatra, but it was Lebanon that invented the temptress. Harlot of the world, Jezebel, was beautiful and knew it and used her (reputedly) many charms to get what she wanted. Nor was she ancient Lebanon's only contribution to aesthetics – Adonis, beloved of Aphrodite and a modern byword for male beauty, was born up in the mountains and lived, loved and died near Qartaba.

Lebanon has more doctors per capita than anywhere else in the Arab World. In fact, it has more doctors per capita than the UK, the US, Canada or Japan. On hospital beds, it doesn't do as well, although it's still the regional leader – the closest competitor being Bahrain. Lebanon ranks 23rd out of 188 countries surveyed on the amount it spends per person on private health care and, as a percentage of the GDP, the amount spent on private and public healthcare is the fifth highest in the world. Life expectancy at birth is 73.4 years, which places Lebanon 11 years behind the world leader, Macau; and Lebanese couples average 2.2 children, which places them ahead of Tunisia (2) but way behind Omani and Yemeni couples, who average 4.9 and 7, respectively.

Were they to come back today, Jezebel and Adonis might well see nothing wrong with their descendents passionate pursuit of beauty by scalpel. What Helena Baroudy or Saniya Habboub Nakkash would have made of it though, is another matter.

Baroudy and Nakkash were pioneers in the field of medicine. Baroudy was the first Lebanese woman to study Western medicine. In fact she was one of the first women to study medicine, for when she travelled to London in the late 1800s to learn, English women had only just been given the right to do so themselves. Baroudy later sat for her license in Istanbul and practiced medicine in a private capacity when she returned to Beirut.

A couple of decades later, Nakkash became the first woman to open her own clinic in Beirut. A graduate of the American Junior College, a forerunner of today's LAU, Nakkash was the first Arab to graduate from the Women's Medical College, now known as Drexel University, in Philadelphia. Returning to Beirut as a qualified obstetrician, she set up her own clinic in 1932 and continued to practice medicine until the early 1980s.

Obesity, if you'll pardon the pun(s), is a big problem in Lebanon. And it's growing. Although it's nowhere near the pandemic it has become in parts of the Gulf – the Kuwaitis, Saudis and Emiratis are in the top 10 in global obesity rankings – it may not be far behind. Two national surveys carried out by the American University in 1997 and 2008 show that, amongst the elderly and the under 20s, obesity has doubled in the last decade and that more than half of those over 20 are overweight. Blame fast cars and even faster food.

Even fifty years ago, this might not have mattered as much. At a time when most people only just got enough to eat, a fuller figure was desirable, a sign of prosperity and good health. These days, a little extra padding is interpreted as slothful, and skinny, yesteryear's indication of poor health, is in. The fuller figured can take heart. Fashion is cyclical. Maybe in a few years, when we've all starved, carved or medicated ourselves to the edge of illness, plump will become the new thin.

SO why are you overweight? Maybe you don't exercise enough. Maybe you work such long hours that you end up eating badly, late at night. Or maybe you find it impossible to say no to another Lahme Beajin and you've never met a Knefe you didn't like. Whatever the reason, you're not happy. What can you do?

You could try surgery. The bariatric band can curb even the most unruly appetite, and modern liposuction techniques can eliminate the most troublesome areas of fat – though at around $1,000 a kilo (or the equivalent cost of 10 kilos of uranium), Lipo isn't cheap.

What if you can't afford the procedure and your bank won't give you a loan? You might try asking your friendly local pharmacist for help.

Diet pills like Xenical, Phen, the infamous Brazilian pill (which like its fore-runners in the 1960s, is amphetamine based and addictive), the attractively-named Starve-Ex and outwardly more healthy-sounding herbal remedies such as Seven Slim Amana, can all be purchased in most Beirut pharmacies without a prescription.

Alternatively, you could just trust your grandmother and drink a teaspoon or two of Apple Vinegar – (Khal il Teffeh) – every morning with your breakfast. Said to be good at breaking down fat, apple vinegar is one of those classic home remedies that's been used to treat allergies, flu, sore throat, arthritis, high cholesterol and acne.

Another miraculous remedy that you'll probably find tucked away somewhere in your kitchen is the black sesame seed, which can be used to treat constipation, nasal congestion, cough, asthma, backache and rheumatism. Oh yes, and it tastes great sprinkled on top of a cake.

L et's not even get started on olive oil. A small glass of it drunk before breakfast will keep you regular and keep the heart healthy. Rubbed on a baby's gums it can help with teething pain (though a dab of brandy is probably more effective and will send the little angel to sleep as well), it soothes and smoothes dry skin, helps prevent wrinkles and can be used to strengthen cuticles and nails. Gently warmed, it can be used to tame unruly hair and repair split ends, while a cotton ball soaked in it and placed in the ear is guaranteed to help you sleep.

A ndy Warhol, like Oscar Wilde, a man known for coining more than his fair share of bon mots, once said that he believed in plastic surgery.

Some people though, believe in it a little too much. Michaela Romanini, Donatella Versace and Jocelyn Wildenstein, aka the Bride of Wildenstein, the wealthy New York socialite who had $4 million worth of surgery and ended up looking like a cat, are all cases in point.

Beirut's designer faces are less extreme. True, the city has its share of surgical excess stories; trout pouts, button-sized snouts and breasts that don't bounce, but for all the accusations of addiction to plastic surgery and a desire to look unreal, Lebanese women are still sensible enough to understand that when it comes to the snip, it s infinitely more preferable to end up looking like Nancy Ajram than Michael Jackson.

But back to the pharmacy. Diet pills aren't the only powerful medical products you can buy over the counter in Beirut. Having trouble sleeping at night and don't fancy soaking your pillow in olive oil? Try Letoxanil. Feeling blue or out of sorts? Prozac or Zoloft should set you right again. Are you awkward in a crowd? Pop a Xanax. Having trouble getting into the mood? Viagra, Levitra and Cialis are all easily available.

From anti-depressants and anti-psychotics to simpler things like hair loss treatments and Botox, there's almost nothing your enterprising local pharmacist can't be persuaded to sell you. The service is so comprehensive that after a while, you might find yourself wondering if you'll ever need a doctor at all.

Nicoderm patches are another popular over-the-counter remedy, though judging by the number of people who still smoke in Beirut, they're probably being used as an extra source of nicotine instead of as a way to stop smoking. Around 3,500 Lebanese die every year of tobacco-related illnesses and over a quarter of all people who die of diseases, over the age of 30, die of tobacco-related conditions like cancer, heart disease and respiratory diseases. No wonder. A study released by the AUB in 2010 showed that 42.9% of Lebanese men and 27.5% of women over 18 smoke cigarettes, 7.8 billion of them a year, or an average of a pack and half a day per smoker. Throw in the arguileh – which the report claims a staggering 60% of kids between the age of 13 and 15 smoke on a regular basis – and that death toll becomes easier to understand.

Lebanon has one of the highest rates of cigarette smoking per capita in the world, but when it comes to following other global trends, it's bang up to date. Beirut may have missed out on following Jane Fonda in going for the burn due to the civil war but the city has made up for lost time and, in recent years, studios offering Yoga, Pilates, Spinning and Tae Bo, have mushroomed all over town.

Working out is not the only modern trend popular in Beirut for those looking for a fast track to the body beautiful. Despite the health risks, including the elevated risk of developing cancer later in life, anabolic steroids like Accutane, MGF, TargeX and HCG are easily available and, as the proliferation of pimples disfiguring well-defined adult backs on beaches up and down the country suggests, they're becoming increasingly popular too.

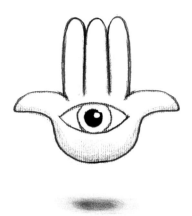

9 BITS & PIECES

From the four things on which all Lebanese agree
and the myriad ways of inviting bad luck to the
places with which Beirut has been compared,
Bits and Pieces is all about fascinating, unusual
and often funny facts we couldn't find place for
anywhere else.

Most people are taught as children not to talk about three things; religion, money and politics. Not in Lebanon. If those three topics were banned, conversation would probably grind to a halt.

There's good reason for the advice. They are amongst the most deeply divisive subjects of conversation, even in the most stable societies. In one where everyone agrees to disagree and people are told that they are all brothers and that they all love one another – sometimes so passionately that the only way they find to express that love is through firearms and RPGs – well, let's just say a frank discussion of any of the three can lead to spectacular results.

Luckily, there's a solution. Enter the jame'a, your gang, a bunch of likeminded individuals who won't be (too) offended by the way you think. If the gulf between public and private discourse can be enormous and even seem somewhat hypocritical, keeping things in the jame'a is the perfect way to let off a little steam and let down your guard without having to worry that what you say might unleash the End of Days – Yom el Iyameh or Il Akhra[1] in Arabic – which is sometimes uttered as a caution in Lebanon – as in Owaak![2], rah Tjeeb Akhirtna – you'll bring about the End of Days/ Hat Ayyem il Iyameh![3]

1- A reference to the destruction (or the end) of the world/ days. Armageddon

2- Beware!

3- You'll bring about our End!

Lebanon's Mediterranean temperament means arguing is a national past time. Explosive shouting matches can be witnessed, or at least overheard, on Beirut's streets every day. Nowhere more so than while driving.

To the uninitiated, the explosive nature of Lebanese arguments can be intimidating. However, navigating them is fairly straightforward and as a broad rule of thumb, the louder and cruder the insults get, the less likely they are to lead to violence.

So you can insult a man by wishing destruction upon his house, you can damn his space or hope that his religion is destroyed. If you want to get more personal, you can inform him that you possess intimate knowledge of his mother, his sister and possibly his father as well. You can accuse him of being a pimp and you can threaten him by saying that if he doesn't back down, you might decide to develop an intimate knowledge of him too.

Two insults, however, are off limits. You may have told a man that his family are all of ill-repute and wished him a lifetime of misery, but call him an animal, or worse still, a donkey and you're guaranteed to get a punch in the face.

They certainly can't agree about which flag to fly during international sporting events. Take the World Cup, for example. In most parts of the world, an event of this magnitude is the cue for local entrepreneurs to start churning out the national flag.

Not here. People may be proud of their lovely cedar flag but come the Cup, you'll have a hard time finding one. Almost overnight, German, Italian, French, Brazilian, Argentinean and even Saudi Arabian flags are draped from windows, attached to cars often in a reckless fashion that suggests the driver doesn't care if he (or you) die! and sported on t-shirts and lapel pins. Nor is the enthusiasm individual. Entire neighbourhoods get caught up in flag fever, competing with each other over who can fly the biggest flag – in some extreme cases the flags are so large, they make the buildings they're attached to look like scale models.

A visitor from space (or anywhere else on earth, for that matter) would be forgiven for thinking that they had taken a wrong turn on the way to Beirut and had landed at the headquarters of the United Nations instead.

Perhaps Lebanon's inhabitants didn't, historically, always leave a great impression of themselves but their country rarely failed to impress. From Biblical times up until the middle of the 20th Century, travellers to Lebanon came away enchanted by its beauty – Ibn Jubair, John Mandeville, Alphonse de Lamartine and Maurice Barres all had lovely things to say about the country.

The violence and horror of the civil war years changed that. Lebanon fell from grace. The conflict was so ferocious that it coined a new adjective – Lebanonization – which came to mean the destruction and division of a country, usually along sectarian lines and was used to describe conflicts in the former Yugoslavia, Afghanistan and Iraq. Meanwhile Beirut, which invariably sent pre-war visitors into raptures, became a universally-accepted shorthand for any kind of urban hell.

Whether you view Lebanon's quarrels as eternal and irresolvable or as simple disagreements between brothers, there are four things on which everyone in Lebanon can agree.

The first is that there is no country more beautiful in the world than Lebanon. The second is the there is no food more delicious than Lebanese food. The third is that there is no singer who sings more beautifully than Fairouz. And the fourth? Well, that's there is no group of people who can agree to agree about less than the Lebanese. Obviously.

Beirut has long since ceased to resemble the images that dominated the world's evening news for so many years. It is twinned with Rio de Janeiro, Quebec, Marseilles, Moscow and Mexico City (despite the oft used comparison to the French capital, Beirut is not twinned with Paris) and regularly features as one of the world's most desirable holiday destinations; but its wartime reputation has proven difficult to shake completely.

From Portland, which George Bush Snr. called Little Beirut after the anti-WTO riots and Chicago, which the Wall Street Journal dubbed Beirut-on-the-lake for its political corruption and violence, Lebanon's lovely capital has been unflatteringly used to describe Daytona Beach (urban blight), Plymouth (violent drunks), Kabul (both for the fighting in the past and now, for the city's nightlife), Glasgow (car thieves), Houston (theft), Hull (for being generally so hellish, most English people wouldn't live there), Montreal (and not because around 100,000 Lebanese live there), Fort Lauderdale (urban blight) and Baltimore (for being the American equivalent of Hull). It even made it into the opening of George Clooney's 2002 film *Welcome to Collinwood* where a billboard welcoming visitors to the ugly, decaying, flyblown city has the "Beirut of Cleveland" scrawled across its front.

There's one other thing (most) Lebanese can agree on; the summer is for making money. Especially out of their brethren from the Arabian Gulf. Prices rise, *Service* miraculously transform into taxis and restaurants discover new and creative ways of padding the bill.

They may not necessarily like being fleeced, but Lebanon's summer guests can take heart in the knowledge that they are in historic company.

Homer thought the Phoenicians wily (when he wasn't calling them lying, cheating scoundrels), Herodotus claimed they stole Greek women and the Romans, who were ruled by three emperors of Levantine birth – Marcus Aurelius Antoninus, who was born in Akkar, Alexander Severus, who was born in Homs and Phillip the Arab, who came from Shahba – accused their eastern Mediterranean citizens of bringing perfumed deceit and oriental decadence to Rome. Quite a charge, especially coming from a city no one could accuse of not knowing its way around an orgy.

or were later visitors much more impressed. European travellers of the 17th, 18th and 19th centuries, who were required to rely on their dragoman guides to get them around the Ottoman Empire in safety, were no more complimentary. Travellers' accounts are full of references to their guides duplicity, flexible morals and their impressive skill at parting their erstwhile employers from their money.

IF some foreigners can't shake the impression that Beirut is still an urban war-zone, it seems that some Beirutis can't either. How else to explain the city's infatuation with fireworks?

Like tourism, Lebanon's peak firework season coincides with the summer. Weddings, religious festivals, a major sporting victory (or even a defeat), the speech of some political leader or simply neighbourhood children lighting firecrackers loud enough to set off car alarms – all excuses to snap, crackle or pop – such that rarely a day goes by without a bang and sometimes so many of them that you'd swear every man, woman and child in the country was setting them off.

Come winter, the fireworks are heard less frequently, at least until the end of the year, when they share the skies with the distinctive red tracer fire from the distinctly Beiruti tradition of welcoming in the New Year in a hail of bullets. Directed (thankfully) at the skies and not at other Beirutis.

You know how in some countries mothers tell their children that it's not nice to talk with their mouths full? Well in Lebanon, that doesn't hold true for talking at the same time as someone else, especially if you both happen to say the same word at the same time. Why? Simply because the one who says the word in question first is guaranteed a longer life than the person they are talking to. This rule holds true unless you both happen to be unmarried women. In this case, you should both pinch each other as quickly as possible because the one who does so first will marry a more handsome husband than the other.

Dreams are confusing things. If you dream of seeing yourself asleep, it means you are going to die. If you dream that your teeth are falling out, it means that someone in your family is about to die. But if you dream about an actual death, it means that the person you are dreaming about is going to have a change of life. Unless that person is you, in which case it doesn't mean anything. Speaking of not meaning anything, dreaming of blood apparently doesn't mean anything either. As long as the blood you dream about is red. If it's any other colour, it means that something really bad is about to happen.

Nor does the *Through The Looking-Glass* fun end there. While some people dream their whole lives of having a boy and are disappointed when they get a girl, dreaming about having a baby boy is a sure sign that trouble is coming; while dreaming about having a baby girl means that you're about to land a windfall. Talk about topsy-turvy.

oud explosions aren't the only things to watch out for in Lebanon. The country's wildlife – and we don't mean Gemmayze on a Saturday night – is also a cause for concern. Did you know, for example that donkeys have been used as suicide bombers? Or that looking an owl in the eyes is certain to get you jinxed?

Then there's the hyena. If you run into one of those – and recent studies show that though they are rare, they still exist, and what's more, can sometimes be found foraging in semi-urban areas – make sure that you run the other way. Quickly. If you don't, the hyena will pee on you, or stare at you with glowing eye (take your pick) in an attempt to mesmerize you. If that happens, you're toast, for the hyena will lure you to its lair where it will be able to eat you in peace.

IT isn't just wild animals that pose a danger. At the very least, domestic cats are not to be trusted. Willing to turn on their owners at a drop of a hat, Beiruti cats have seven spirits (which makes them devilishly difficult to kill) and are very jealous of children, especially young babies. They also have a taste for dead men's eyes, which is why it's important never to leave a corpse unguarded. Haters beware. Cats have a direct line to God. Harm one in anyway and it can bring the wrath of Heaven to bear upon you and may even guarantee you a one-way ticket to Hell.

Harming cats aside, there are plenty of other ways of guaranteeing yourself, or someone else, a bit of bad luck. Wearing your shirt inside out? Bad luck. Hear a humming sound in your ears? Someone's saying something unpleasant about you. Bad luck. Got vines or other creepers growing on the walls or roof of your house? The life's being sucked out of you. Probably not a good thing. Talking about cancer and called it by its name instead of calling it that disease? You've invited sickness upon yourself. Just met someone with blue eyes and a gap between their teeth? You're probably already under the evil eye. Complimented a friend or a loved one without knocking on wood, saying Ism al Salib or Yighzi al Ain afterwards? This one's slightly better, but only in the sense that you've just cast the evil eye on them, rather than yourself.

IT goes without saying that good luck is somewhat harder to come by, though it's by no means impossible. Bite your tongue by mistake for example and you can at least take solace in the knowledge that you're about to receive a gift of some kind. Similarly, the next time your left hand starts itching, resist the urge to scratch and take heart, it's a sign that money is winging its way towards you. If it's your right hand, though, then trouble is looming. It's believed to be a sure sign that you're about to hit someone.

D eath is somewhere in between. Not as easy to invite as bad luck, it's still easier to invite than good luck. Open your umbrella in the house and someone in your family will die. Cut your nails at night and you shorten your own life. If you hear a dog howling during the night, immediately turn your slippers face up, otherwise you invite bad luck and the possibility that someone you know will die. Beware though. It's only acceptable to turn your slippers upside down after hearing a dog howl. At any other time, you risk offending God. Which may also hasten your death. Finally, never go out immediately after taking a shower. It may not lead directly to your death, (though you'd be forgiven for thinking it will, given the impassioned imprecations you'll hear from concerned relatives) but it will certainly make you sick. The warning is specific to showers, though, so going outside after a hammam or a bath is just fine.

Teach your children never to eat eggs in hot weather, unless they want to get acne. Tell them not to eat Za'atar before they go to bed, because it will keep them awake but remind them to eat plenty of Za'atar before an exam, as it will help them remember everything they studied. Unless their exam is first thing in the morning, in which case they might remember everything they studied but find themselves unable to keep their eyes open during the exam because they didn't sleep the night before.

Tell them never to eat fish and dairy products within three hours of each other because it causes food poisoning; as good a reason as any to steer clear of the McFillet-O-Fish. Never allow them to eat food that's fallen on the floor because it's been touched by the devil. It's probably not clean either, but the devil bit sounds more dramatic. Finally, if they choke while they're eating, look around the room. Someone there is jealous of what they are eating and is casting the evil eye. Unless they're eating the aforementioned McFillet, in which case the choking is probably the natural reaction to putting it in their mouth in the first place.

IF you arrive at someone's house and find that there's coffee already prepared for you, take heart; it means that your mother-in-law loves you. Unless the house in question is your mother-in-law's, in which case she was probably expecting you because your spouse called ahead. In this case, arriving to find the coffee already made may still mean that your mother-in-law loves you, but it might also mean that she doesn't like you one little bit, but, as she can't tell your spouse that without causing a huge problem, she's made the coffee before you get there to be able to get you out of her house as quickly as is politely possible.

E ven assuming the child is born with a healthy appetite for the foods that are good for it, there are still a couple of things you need to take care of if your baby is to grow up tall and strong. The first thing is to make sure no one ever steps over him or her by mistake because if that happens, the child's growth is sure to be stunted. (For the cure to this ailment, see chapter 7.) Similarly, it's also important that when you put your child to bed, you teach them to sleep with their legs straight and not curled behind them. If they don't, they will eventually stop growing. Parents of Beirut beware, if your child doesn't grow big and tall, it's no one's fault but your own.

Speaking of babies, it seems that the ability to make their daughter-in-laws' lives a misery isn't a mother-in-law's only super power. They can also tell, when their son's wife gets pregnant, whether the child will be a boy or girl. As for the mother-to-be, she shouldn't wear lipstick unless she wants her baby to be born with intensely red lips – a real handicap for a boy but presumably not as much of a problem for a Lebanese girl. The moral of these two stories? A pregnant woman should probably not wear make-up but if she does, she should at least consult her mother-in-law before deciding whether to put on any lipstick.

Other old wives tales make even less sense. Deny a pregnant woman make-up perhaps, but always give her whatever kind of food she desires. If you do not do so, her baby will apparently grow up with an intense longing for the food its mother was denied. Of course, were one to follow this peculiar logic through to its end, it would make sense – for the future baby, anyway – to deny a pregnant woman fresh vegetables, fruit or any of the healthy food we are all supposed to eat but find excuses to avoid, especially as children.